LET'S TALK ABOUT

TEMPLES AND RITUAL

OTHER BOOKS IN THE
LET'S TALK ABOUT SERIES

Let's Talk about Polygamy

Let's Talk about Religion and Mental Health

Let's Talk about the Book of Abraham

Let's Talk about the Law of Consecration

Let's Talk about Faith and Intellect

*Let's Talk about the Translation
of the Book of Mormon*

Let's Talk about Race and Priesthood

For more information on the other books
in the Let's Talk About series,
visit DesBook.com/LetsTalk.

LET'S TALK ABOUT

TEMPLES AND RITUAL

JENNIFER C. LANE

SALT LAKE CITY, UTAH

Quote on page 92: "Awake and Arise" by Theodore E. Curtis © by Intellectual Reserve, Inc.

© 2023 Jennifer C. Lane

All rights reserved. No part of this book may be reproduced in any form or by any means without permission in writing from the publisher, Deseret Book Company, at permissions@deseretbook.com. This work is not an official publication of The Church of Jesus Christ of Latter-day Saints. The views expressed herein are the responsibility of the author and do not necessarily represent the position of the Church or of Deseret Book Company.

DESERET BOOK is a registered trademark of Deseret Book Company.

Visit us at deseretbook.com

Library of Congress Cataloging-in-Publication Data
Names: Lane, Jennifer C., 1968– author.
Title: Let's talk about temples and ritual / Jennifer C. Lane.
Other titles: Let's talk about (Deseret Book)
Description: Salt Lake City, Utah: Deseret Book, [2023] | Series: Let's talk about | Includes bibliographical references and index. | Summary: "Author and educator Jennifer C. Lane explains temple worship and ritual in The Church of Jesus Christ of Latter-day Saints"—Provided by publisher.
Identifiers: LCCN 2022045963 | ISBN 9781639931200 (trade paperback)
Subjects: LCSH: The Church of Jesus Christ of Latter-day Saints—Rituals. | Mormon temples. | Mormon Church—Rituals.
Classification: LCC BX8643. T4 L36 2023 | DDC 246/.9589332—dc23/eng/20221117
LC record available at https://lccn.loc.gov/2022045963

Printed in the United States of America
University Press, Provo, UT

10 9 8 7 6 5 4 3

*For my grandparents,
whose faithful temple service
pointed me to Christ*

CONTENTS

Introduction 1

1. Leaving the World: Holiness to the Lord 5
2. Becoming His: Children of the Covenant 15
3. The House of the Lord: A Home for the Lord in Our Day 23
4. Ritual Orientation: Sacred Time and Space 32
5. The Journey: Continuing on the Covenant Path . . 47
6. New Identity: Putting On Christ 55
7. Redemption: Entering the Presence of the Lord . . 65
8. The Gift: Endowment of Power 73
9. God's Order: The New and Everlasting Covenant . 83
10. The Plan: All Invited Home 92
11. The Way: Knowing the Lord 103

Acknowledgments 117

Further Reading 119

Notes 121

Index 127

INTRODUCTION

The temple is a vast and deep topic, and this is a short book. I cannot tell or even summarize all the profound insights that many have shared through the years. I hope to do two things with the time that we have together. I want to share how I have come to see and experience redemption through Christ in the temple in hopes that others might experience that more fully as well, and I want to speak to concerns or questions that might keep someone from feeling to sing the song of redeeming love in relation to the temple. I will try to do the two hand in hand.

Each chapter of this book addresses a question and is a piece of a picture that depicts how Christ invites us to come unto Him and be perfected in Him through the ordinances and covenants of the temple. In composing that image, I will use many smaller pieces of history and scripture analysis that I have expanded or could expand into books of their own. These pieces layer together, sometimes overlapping, and build up to create a larger picture of how the temple brings us to Christ and the eternal life that He offers.

Questions are important. They are how we learn. They are part of our effort to receive answers from the Lord. I may not have the exact answer that you or someone you know is looking for, but I want to share answers that have helped me. The Old Testament tabernacle was known as the "tent of the congregation," which can also be translated as the "tent of meeting" (see Exodus 40:2, NIV). As we seek to *meet* the Lord in

His house, we can find help and answers to questions deep in our hearts. The temples of the Restoration also extend a question to us, an invitation to find Christ, learn of Him, and experience the abundant life that He provides.

The temple is key to accepting the invitation to come unto Christ. It is how we come to know Him as we become more like Him. In the past, President Lorenzo Snow helped the Church see the urgency of paying tithing, President Heber J. Grant explained how serious the expectation of the Word of Wisdom was, President David O. McKay clarified the need for every member to be a missionary, and President Ezra Taft Benson taught how daily study of the Book of Mormon helps us come unto Christ; similarly, in our day, President Russell M. Nelson has helped us see the vital role of temple ordinances in moving us forward on the covenant path. He has helped us see how the gathering of Israel is a gathering to the temple, on both sides of the veil.

In the last days, the Lord seeks to gather His covenant people and "[restore] all the house of Jacob unto the knowledge of the covenant that he hath covenanted with them" so that we can "know [our] Redeemer, who is Jesus Christ, the Son of God" (3 Nephi 5:25–26). I hope that these reflections on the temple and temple ritual will provide some resources for your own journey of learning and growth. I know that He invites us to walk His covenant path as we prepare to return to His presence.

INTRODUCTION

Questions Answered in This Book

Chapter 1, "Leaving the World: Holiness to the Lord"
- Why do we build temples?
- Why can't everyone enter the temple?
- Why do we need a temple recommend?
- How is the temple today similar to and different from Old Testament temples?

Chapter 2, "Becoming His: Children of the Covenant"
- Why do temple covenants matter? How do they change my relationship with the Lord?

Chapter 3, "The House of the Lord: A Home for the Lord in Our Day"
- What does the Restoration teach about the need for temples in our day?
- How does the Lord manifest Himself in His house?

Chapter 4, "Ritual Orientation: Sacred Time and Space"
- Why does the formal ritual worship in the temple differ so much from our weekly Sunday meetings?
- How is learning from ritual different than getting information from a lecture?

Chapter 5, "The Journey: Continuing on the Covenant Path"
- How does the temple connect to the doctrine of Christ?
- How can we feel confident making additional covenants in the temple when we know that we are weak?

Chapter 6, "New Identity: Putting On Christ"
- What is the significance of wearing the temple garment?
- In what ways does it protect us?

Chapter 7, "Redemption: Entering the Presence of the Lord"
- How can I make sense of possible ties between temple practices and the ritual practices of Freemasonry?

- What is the message conveyed in the presentation of the endowment?

Chapter 8, "The Gift: Endowment of Power"
- Why have there been changes in the endowment ceremony over time?
- What is the "gift" that the endowment gives us?

Chapter 9, "God's Order: The New and Everlasting Covenant"
- How can we understand temple marriage as part of the covenant path when many do not have the opportunity or desire for this kind of marriage in mortality?

Chapter 10, "The Plan: All Invited Home"
- Why are we trying to perform ordinances for everyone who has ever lived?
- What is the relationship of Christ's Atonement, vicarious ordinances, and agency?

Chapter 11, "The Way: Knowing the Lord"
- Why should we return to serve in the temple as often as our circumstances permit?

CHAPTER 1

LEAVING THE WORLD: HOLINESS TO THE LORD

> *"No more a stranger, or a guest,*
> *But like a child at home."*
>
> —Isaac Watts, "My Shepherd Will Supply My Need"

I served as a missionary in France, and my first area was close to the Spanish border. Sometimes we contacted people along a walkway with a beautiful view of the Pyrenees Mountains. One day shortly after I arrived, we talked with a woman from Germany. Since I can remember much of the conversation, we must have been speaking in English. She had heard of The Church of Jesus Christ of Latter-day Saints but couldn't understand why we spent money to build temples. Nothing we said seemed to help her understand.

I would often refer to this experience when teaching a New Testament class at BYU–Hawaii. In John 12, Mary the sister of Martha anointed Christ with very precious ointment. Judas asked, "Why was not this ointment sold for three hundred pence, and given to the poor?" (v. 5). Christ did not say that the needs of the poor did not matter but that "the poor always ye have with you; but me ye have not always" (v. 8). Caring for those in need is a constant obligation of disciples, but sometimes resources are also needed for worshipping of the Savior. Christ pointed to this anointing as having been done "against the day of my burying" (v. 7). There was a ritual dimension of anointing, both for burial and for anointing the kings of Israel. That week before His death, Christ was to come into Jerusalem as the King of Israel.

As with the anointing of Christ, we use Church resources for temples in which we experience sacred rituals and worship God. Being connected with Christ more fully, we can more fully serve our neighbors and those in need. In temples and temple ritual we are invited into God's world, His realm or kingdom. In them we come unto Christ. As we worship Christ and the Father in temples, we move away from world-oriented lives and values. Christ taught, "Where your treasure is, there will your heart be also" (Matthew 6:21). We choose our treasure first. Then that treasure, what we choose to value, resets our hearts. We recalibrate ourselves as we invest our time and treasure. Choosing to worship in temples is choosing to focus our hearts on Christ.

The modern world has any number of places that orient us and put us within a larger story of who we are and what matters in life. Billions of dollars are spent on sports teams and arenas, movies and movie theaters. The narratives that we participate in at stadiums, theaters, shopping malls, museums, and amusement parks all tell a story about who we are and what matters in life, whether that is having the latest fashion, being number one, or living a life of excitement or romance.

Our time in these places shapes our lives and turns our hearts and minds, changing what we become. This shift can occur even without leaving our homes. Our participation in digital spaces orients us and tells us how we fit into a larger reality. With social media, video games, and streaming shows, we enter into a version of reality as we play and consume. The more we participate, the more at home we feel in these worlds.

In the temple of His restored Church, Christ invites us to join Him in His world of holiness and godliness. It's a change to be in that sacred place, leaving the secular world that we live in. One might initially feel disoriented when receiving the endowment. I remember a Church member on my mission telling me that as she received her endowment, she didn't feel like she understood. She decided that the way to learn was to keep going, and so she turned around and attended the next session. With time, we can come to see that temples help us learn and live a different story, one focused on seeking God's presence. We learn of His plan to create a world for us, to give us opportunities to grow, to receive the blessings of Christ's Atonement, and to become holy and prepared to return home again.

A longing for a place of holiness is not unique to Latter-day Saints; throughout history people have sought places with more than what the world offers. The Lord reveals His truths to speak to that human longing, and He gives us temples so we can have the means to come unto Him: "Whenever the Lord has had a people on the earth who will obey His word, they have been commanded to build temples."[1]

Holiness for the Lord's People

As we think about why we need temples and why there is a process of interviews to receive a temple recommend, the experience of the children of Israel can help us identify a pattern. After bringing the children of Israel out of their bondage in Egypt, the Lord Jehovah sought to covenant with all of Israel, to make them a holy people, His kingdom of priests and priestesses to bless the entire world. "Ye have seen what I did unto the Egyptians, and how I bare you on eagles' wings, and brought you unto myself. Now therefore, if ye will obey my voice indeed, and keep my covenant, then ye shall be a peculiar treasure unto me above all people: for all the earth is mine: And ye shall be unto me a kingdom of priests, and an holy nation" (Exodus 19:4–6). The Lord is holy, and we must be holy to be with Him. No unclean thing can dwell in the presence of God or enter into His kingdom (see 1 Nephi 10:21; 3 Nephi 27:19).

Our efforts to live holy lives prepare us to be worthy to enter the temple. These efforts are certified by our being interviewed and found worthy to hold a temple recommend. In the words of Elder Ronald A. Rasband, holding a recommend indicates that we are "recommended to the Lord." He noted that "the temple is the Lord's house and a sanctuary from the world. His Spirit envelops those who worship within those sacred walls. He sets the standards by which we enter as His guests."[2]

In gathering Israel in our day, we invite all to come and join us as we journey back to God. "Just to be clear," Sister Reyna I. Aburto explained, speaking of the temple recommend, "it's not that we want to keep the people out. It is just that it takes a special journey to be here. And this is a journey of change, a journey of devotion and of love."[3] Making and keeping the initial covenant of baptism is preparation for attending the temple. The year of waiting between an adult being baptized and being able to receive his or her endowment points to the growth and maturity that comes as we learn to walk on the covenant path before taking on new covenant obligations.

We leave the world and seek to be holy to enter the Lord's house as we keep our baptismal covenants with our continued faith and repentance. We continue to become clean and holy through daily repentance, partaking of the sacrament, and feeling the sanctifying influence of the Holy Ghost.

Holiness in Temple Structure

We see this pattern of seeking holiness in the Old Testament. The children of Israel knew it was important to be holy for the Lord to be among them. In the symbols and structure of the Old Testament temple, with its Levitical, or Aaronic, Priesthood ordinances, God's holiness was revealed. Not just

LEAVING THE WORLD: HOLINESS TO THE LORD

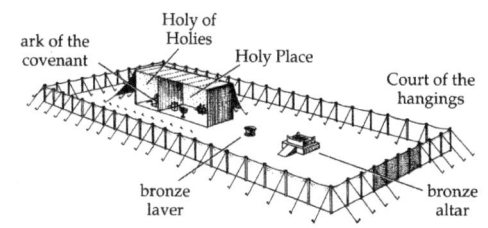

Tent of Meeting, by Michael P. Lyon

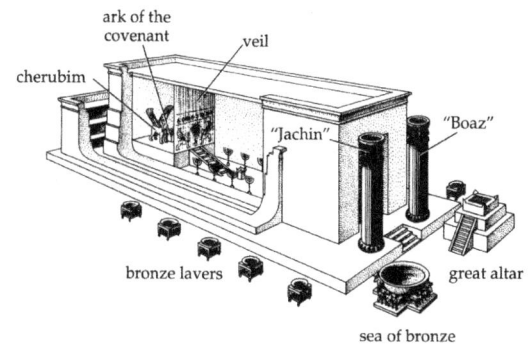

Temple of Solomon, by Michael P. Lyon

anyone could enter. Most of the temple area was reserved only for the priests and Levites. In fact, there were levels of holiness; some places were so holy that they were rarely approached and only with special preparation. Our temple today is not this kind of Aaronic or Levitical temple, but the Old Testament temple provides types and shadows of eternal spiritual truth.

In Old Testament temples there was first a courtyard with a wall that separated the temple from the outside world and profane space. Within the courtyard was an altar with fire, upon which sacrifices were cooked. Beyond the altar was the "laver," a font of water in which the priests would wash themselves to be ritually pure before approaching the Lord's presence. In Solomon's temple a metal laver was set on the backs of twelve oxen, just as the baptismal fonts in our temple baptistries are. The images of fire and water symbolize how we are spiritually cleansed to be in the presence of God.

The temple building (or tent of the tabernacle) in the middle of the courtyard had two rooms. The first room was the Holy Place, where only the priests could enter. In this outer room the priests kept the incense altar and candelabra burning and weekly brought the holy shewbread. The candelabra's light represented God's glory. The incense altar stood before the veil, and the rising smoke of the incense represented prayers ascending to God.

Beyond the Holy Place, behind a veil separating the two rooms, was the Holy of Holies, or Most Holy Place, where the ark of the covenant stood. Within the ark of the covenant were kept the tablets with the law, a pot of manna, and Aaron's rod. They reminded the people of all that the Lord had done for them and that they were the Lord's covenant people. This room served as God's throne room on earth.

The Holy of Holies could be entered only by the high priest and only on the Day of Atonement. The high priest would come with blood to be placed on the mercy seat (ark of the covenant). This made an atonement for all of Israel, foreshadowing Christ's role as the Great High Priest (see Leviticus 16:14–19; Hebrews 9:11–15).

Passing into God's presence through the veil also pointed to Christ, who opens our access to God; the temple veil was rent at His death (see Mark 15:38). Though only the high priest could go through the veil to the Holy of Holies and only on the Day of Atonement, we can have "boldness to enter into the holiest by the blood of Jesus, by a new and living way, which he hath consecrated for us, through the veil, that is to say, his flesh" (Hebrews 10:19–20). Just as the structure of the

LEAVING THE WORLD: HOLINESS TO THE LORD

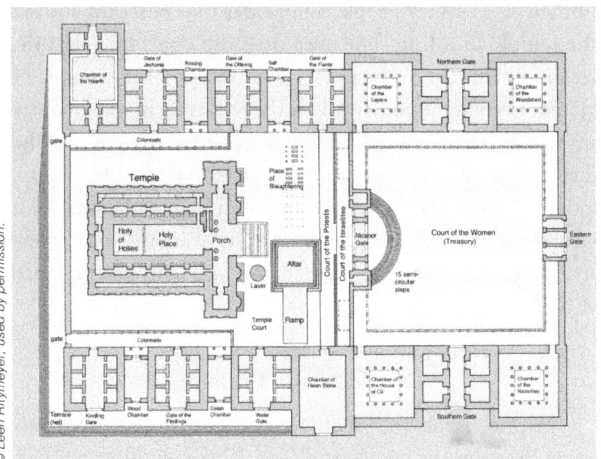

Plan of the Herodian Temple Complex, by Leen Ritmeyer

ancient temple modeled for the ancient Israelites the increasing holiness needed to enter God's presence, the endowment ceremony illustrates how, as we become holier through Christ, we come closer to the Lord and symbolically enter into His presence.

All Are Invited into His Presence

As the Israelites came toward the temple, they left the world behind. "Who shall ascend into the hill of the Lord? or who shall stand in his holy place? He that hath clean hands, and a pure heart; who hath not lifted up his soul unto vanity, nor sworn deceitfully" (Psalm 24:3–4). Approaching the presence of God required holiness for all, but there was an extra level of expectations for the priests. The priests represented the Lord, and so they needed to purify themselves before helping others approach His presence by offering sacrifices on their behalf.

Although the Israelites came to the temple to seek the presence of the Lord, if they were not priests, they could not enter the actual building of the temple or the tent of the tabernacle.

Initially it seems lay people could enter the courtyard around the temple building, but over time the courtyard was increasingly limited to the priests and Levites. In the temple of Herod, beyond the courtyard for the priests there was an outer courtyard for men and, farther out, one for women. Unlike then, when only male descendants of Aaron could be priests, today all can enter the temple and both men and women are set apart with priesthood authority to serve as ordinance workers. We are all invited to become holy and enter the presence of God.

Holiness and Wholeness through Offerings and Rituals

The priests' role was to offer sacrifices to provide reconciliation between the people and God. These sacrifices pointed to Christ and His doctrine. Representing the Savior Himself, the priests helped make atonement for repentant people who brought offerings to be sacrificed: "The priest shall make an atonement for them, and it shall be forgiven them" (Leviticus 4:20). The symbolic actions of the priests in this process of sacrifice can be described as "rites" or "ritual actions." Another word for *rite* or *ritual* is *ordinance*. President Boyd K. Packer explained that "the word *ordinance* means, 'religious ceremonial observance'; 'an established rite.'"[4] Through these ceremonial and sacred temple rituals (ordinances), the people sought to become holy and draw closer to the Lord.

The death of the animal and the application of blood in many of these offerings pointed to Christ's atoning blood, which through the ordinances of our day, cleanses us and makes us worthy to be in His presence. Cleansing also speaks to the healing and wholeness that Christ brings us as we move from a worldly way of life to becoming more fully integrated into God's life of wholeness and holiness. In the sacrifices' role to bring reconciliation and "at-one-ment," we see a type of Christ.

LEAVING THE WORLD: HOLINESS TO THE LORD

In our day, as in ancient days, the temple rituals point us to Christ and His atoning sacrifice. In the ordinance of the endowment today, we symbolically become increasingly holy as we ritually embody Christ, as did the priests. Likewise, in the temple ordinances, we ritually offer our willingness to become like Him and we ritually receive the gifts of Christ's atoning sacrifice. As Elder Jeffrey R. Holland reminded us, "The temple is His house, and He should be uppermost in our minds and hearts—the majestic doctrine of Christ pervading our very being just as it pervades the temple ordinances—from the time we read the inscription over the front door to the very last moment we spend in the building. Amid all the wonder we encounter, we are to see, above all else, the meaning of Jesus in the temple."[5]

Christ and the Temple

During His ministry, Christ Himself worshipped at the temple, but He also repeatedly taught that the temple pointed to Him. In John 7 and 8, we see Christ at the temple on the Feast of Sukkot, or Tabernacles. He compared Himself to the light of the temple that was set up in the courtyard ("I am the light of the world: he that followeth me shall not walk in darkness, but shall have the light of life" [8:12]) and also to the water that was poured out on the altar by the high priest ("If any man thirst, let him come unto me, and drink" [7:37]). The light and life associated with the temple through these symbols pointed to Him. As King Benjamin taught, Christ is the Lord God Omnipotent who came to dwell in a tabernacle of clay just as He had dwelt in a tabernacle in the wilderness and the temple in Israel (see Mosiah 3:5).

Over time most Christians came to believe that the coming of Christ fulfilled the need for a house of the Lord. The temple was destroyed by the Romans in AD 70. In our day, a Jewish synagogue is sometimes called a "temple," and there

LET'S TALK ABOUT TEMPLES AND RITUAL

are still some Jewish people who look forward to a day when the temple will be rebuilt. Most Jews and Christians, however, generally see the temple as something belonging to biblical times. This is part of why, as a Church, we are unusual in building temples. Most Christians' understanding is that because Christ came in the flesh and "tabernacled among us" (John 1:14, TLV), the temple symbolism of the house of the Lord is fulfilled; a physical building is no longer needed. They believe that the Lord continues to be with His people in the bodily temple of the believers, His Church, through His Spirit.

But with the Restoration of Christ's Church came a new sense of how immediately and tangibly the Lord seeks to manifest Himself to His people through covenants and ordinances. Just as through the ordinance of the sacrament we can see Christ, who died to give us life, and partake of the emblems of His body and blood, in the ordinances of the temple we can behold Christ's gift of His atoning sacrifice. In His postmortal ministries, He invited people to come unto Him individually and to know Him for themselves by feeling the wounds in His hands and feet. In the ordinances we can have a similar experience of witnessing Him and entering into His presence.

In the temple, as we covenant to become His children, we accept His invitation to "return unto [Him], and repent of [our] sins, and be converted, that [He] may heal [us]" (3 Nephi 9:13). In the ordinances of the temple, we can reach out and accept the arm of mercy He extends: "If ye will come unto me ye shall have eternal life. Behold, mine arm of mercy is extended towards you, and whosoever will come, him will I receive; and blessed are those who come unto me" (3 Nephi 9:14).

CHAPTER 2

BECOMING HIS: CHILDREN OF THE COVENANT

"Redeemer of Israel,
Our only delight,
On whom for a blessing we call,
Our shadow by day
And our pillar by night,
Our King, our Deliv'rer, our all!"

—William W. Phelps, "Redeemer of Israel"

In addition to bringing a restored sense of how important a physical temple is, the Restoration highlights the importance of covenants in the Father's plan to bring us back to Him. While many religious truths were preserved in the years after Christ was on the earth, the importance of covenants was lost (see 1 Nephi 13:26). Without an understanding of covenants, the importance of the temple was also lost.

The Bible records how the house of Israel covenanted with the Lord at Sinai and worshipped in the temple, but this covenant was not the higher covenant of earlier days. In our day, the Lord did not restore the temple of the law of Moses, with the outward sacrifices of the Levitical or Aaronic Priesthood. Instead, in modern temples, with the ordinances of the endowment and sealing, we participate in the higher, Melchizedek Priesthood covenants and worship that the ancient patriarchs and matriarchs performed.

Creating covenant relationships is central to the Father's plan of redemption and the primary function of the temple. President Russell M. Nelson explained: "*Everything* we believe and *every* promise God has made to His covenant people come together in the temple. In *every* age, the temple has underscored the precious truth that those who make covenants with God and keep them are children of the covenant. Thus, in the house of the Lord, we can make the same covenants with God that Abraham, Isaac, and Jacob made. And we can receive the same blessings!"[1] In the temple, the Lord offers us the fullness of His covenant promises and blessings.

Ancient Covenants and New Names

Today, we often associate covenants with contracts, impersonal agreements between people. Anciently, however, covenants were much more personal. In the Church we know that we make promises to God with our covenants, and God, in turn, makes promises to us. As we understand the ancient sense of a covenant, these promises take on a deeper meaning.

In the ancient world, covenants weren't just a series of promises but were used to create new relationships, like adoption or marriage. Covenants made in sacred places created a new family relationship with the Lord. Individuals like Abram and Sarai responded to God's invitation to create that relationship. This new relationship was often characterized by a new name, like Abraham or Sarah, that reflected the new status—Abraham, "father of many nations," or Sarah, "princess."

Names in the ancient world indicated one's nature. At Peniel, Jacob was told: "Thy name shall be called no more Jacob, but Israel: for as a prince hast thou power with God and with men, and hast prevailed" (Genesis 32:28). With a new relationship, the potential for a new nature was opened up. We see an example of this covenant identity and potential in the new names of the patriarchs and matriarchs.

BECOMING HIS: CHILDREN OF THE COVENANT

Through covenant, their identity and purpose were transformed. They were given power to become more godly. Abram became Abraham: an exalted father became a father of many nations. Abraham may not have immediately become what his name indicated—in fact, at one point he faced the possibility that his sacrifice and obedience would mean the death of his covenant son—but he had a sense of what he would become through covenant faithfulness.

The places where these new relationships were created became sacred spaces. God revealed not only the new identity of people with their new names but also His own identity and name in these places. After being given the name Israel, Jacob asked, "Tell me, I pray thee, thy name. And he said, Wherefore is it that thou dost ask after my name? And he blessed him there. And Jacob called the name of the place Peniel: for I have seen God face to face, and my life is preserved" (Genesis 32:29–30).

Moses, on Horeb, the mountain of God, similarly saw God and learned of His name and nature. After being given his mission, Moses asked: "Behold, when I come unto the children of Israel, and shall say unto them, The God of your fathers hath sent me unto you; and they shall say to me, What is his name? what shall I say unto them? And God said unto Moses, I Am That I Am: and he said, Thus shalt thou say unto the children of Israel, I Am hath sent me unto you" (Exodus 3:13–14).

Temples are places to meet God, places to create covenant relationships, places where God can reveal Himself to us and help us take on His name and nature. In times before a temple could be built, God revealed Himself in sacred places, such as Mount Horeb or the Sacred Grove. Yet these appearances were always preparatory to establishing a people who could build a house so "that the Son of Man might have a place to manifest himself to his people" (Doctrine and Covenants 109:5).

LET'S TALK ABOUT TEMPLES AND RITUAL

Covenants and Redemption

Through these covenants with the Lord Jehovah (the premortal Jesus Christ), Abraham and Sarah, Isaac and Rebecca, and Jacob and Rachel entered a new relationship with Him. They became His spiritual children, and He became their spiritual father. It is this covenant connection that the Lord wanted to return to the earth in our day to allow us to more fully live lives of holiness and be prepared to return to His presence.

We see this pattern of making covenants to create a family relationship so that we can be redeemed in Mosiah 5: "Because of the covenant which ye have made ye shall be called the children of Christ, his sons, and his daughters; for behold, this day he hath spiritually begotten you; for ye say that your hearts are changed through faith on his name; therefore, ye are born of him and have become his sons and his daughters" (v. 7). Through covenant we become the children of covenant with Christ. Covenants are central to the plan of redemption and a vital part of why the construction of temples is so important in our day.

The Lord explains in scripture that He redeemed the children of Israel from their bondage in Egypt because of the covenant He had made with Abraham, Isaac, and Jacob (see Exodus 6:3–6; Deuteronomy 7:8; 1 Nephi 17:40). This type of family relationship, with the Lord as their Redeemer, was understood in the ancient world. Among the Israelites, the father or oldest male relative had obligations as a *gō'ēl*. A *gō'ēl*, best translated as "kinsman-redeemer," had the responsibility to buy family members out of bondage. Likewise, through covenants with Abraham, Isaac, and Jacob, the Lord became their *gō'ēl*, the Kinsman-Redeemer of Israel.

A great blessing of covenants being restored in our day is creating a relationship with the Lord Jehovah so that He will be our spiritual Father, our *gō'ēl*. As children of the covenant, we have a Kinsman-Redeemer who can redeem us from the bondage of sinful ways of living and thinking. Through His redeeming power we can live lives of holiness far beyond what we could on our own.

Our covenant creates a new family relationship, and this relationship with the Lord makes our spiritual redemption possible. "And under this head ye are made free, and there is no other head whereby ye can be made free. There is no other name given whereby salvation cometh; therefore, I would that ye should take upon you the name of Christ, all you that have entered into the covenant with God that ye should be obedient unto the end of your lives" (Mosiah 5:8).

Elder David A. Bednar explained how the temple ordinances are a continuation of creating this covenant relationship with the Lord:

> The process of taking upon ourselves the name of Jesus Christ that is commenced in the waters of baptism is continued and enlarged in the house of the Lord. As we stand in the waters of baptism, we look to the temple. As we partake of the sacrament, we look to the temple. We pledge to always remember the Savior and to keep His commandments as preparation to participate in the sacred ordinances of the temple and receive the highest blessings available through the name and by the authority of the Lord Jesus Christ. Thus, in the ordinances of the holy temple we more completely and fully take upon us the name of Jesus Christ.[2]

Like the ancient patriarchs and matriarchs, we receive a new name with our covenants to indicate the new nature and relationship that we are taking on. As part of our covenant redemption, we also take upon us the name and nature of Christ. We are endowed so that as His "servants [we] may go forth from this house armed with [His] power, and that [His] name may be upon [us], and [His] glory be round about

[us], and [His] angels have charge over [us]" (Doctrine and Covenants 109:22). Through this covenant relationship we are redeemed from the bondage of sin, endowed with power, and restored to the presence of God.

The Rest of the Lord

Because of the covenant relationship of Abraham, Isaac, and Jacob, God was able to fully reveal Himself to them in ancient days. Their covenants helped them become holy enough to enter into His presence. We learn in the Doctrine and Covenants that the Lord wanted to give these higher Melchizedek Priesthood covenants, the endowment, to the children of Israel at Sinai so they could all enter into His presence, but they were not willing to receive them. Moses "sought diligently to sanctify his people that they might behold the face of God; But they hardened their hearts and could not endure his presence; therefore, the Lord in his wrath, for his anger was kindled against them, swore that they should not enter into his rest while in the wilderness, which rest is the fulness of his glory" (Doctrine and Covenants 84:23–24).

The house of Israel was left with the lesser covenant of the law of Moses, and with this lower covenant they were kept further from His presence. We can see that distance in the design of the Old Testament temple with its Levitical or Aaronic Priesthood ordinances. With these lesser priesthood ordinances, only the high priest could enter into the Holy of Holies, the presence of the Lord, and only on one day of the year.

Moses had tried to teach the children of Israel that "no man can see the face of God, even the Father, and live" without the ordinances of the greater priesthood, or Melchizedek Priesthood (Doctrine and Covenants 84:22). Known as the "provocation in the wilderness," the Israelites' unwillingness to receive the blessings of the Melchizedek Priesthood ordinances kept them from experiencing the fullness of God's presence, His rest. In the Book of Mormon, Jacob worried this would happen to his people: "Wherefore we labored diligently among our people, that we might persuade them to come unto Christ, and partake of the goodness of God, that they might enter into his rest, lest by any means he should swear in his wrath they should not enter in, as in the provocation in the days of temptation while the children of Israel were in the wilderness" (Jacob 1:7).

In the latter days, the Restoration reestablished the covenants given to Abraham, Isaac, and Jacob. With the Melchizedek Priesthood once again on the earth in our day, we are able to experience His presence through the gift of the Holy Ghost. In the temple, we can receive the fullness of the Holy Ghost through the Melchizedek Priesthood temple ordinances (see Doctrine and Covenants 109:15). Every time we make and keep covenants, we are choosing to "come unto Christ, and partake of the goodness of God, that [we] might enter into his rest." In our day He invites us to His house to find rest in Him. The temple provides a spiritual home in which we can grow, learn, and be prepared for our work in the world. The Lord invites us to His home, the temple, to learn of Him and to come to know Him more fully.

The ordinances of the temple help us learn how to come unto Christ, thereby becoming more like Him while facing life's challenges. Life can be hard, and we need places of refuge to rest and recharge as we continue on our mortal journeys.

Over twenty years ago, I learned that my mother had only a few days left to live. Before we flew to Southern California to see her, my husband and I attended an endowment session in the Laie Hawaii Temple. I spoke with my brother and sister-in-law afterward, and they too had attended a session, in the Oakland Temple, before they left to see her one last time. We had all cried as we prayed in the temple, but we felt peace. We were reassured by the eternal perspective provided through the presentation of the endowment, which showed us the purpose of Creation and our life on earth and the role of Christ in bringing us back home again. With this perspective, knowing that our mother had made and kept her covenants, we were prepared to say a temporary goodbye.

In the house of the Lord, we briefly leave the stresses and worries of our daily lives so that we can receive spiritual orientation and power to continue our journey back to God. Being in the temple prepares us for living in the world as the Lord's representatives. Elder Bednar explained, "We do not come to the temple to hide from or escape the evils of the world. Rather, we come to the temple to conquer the world of evil. As we invite into our lives the 'power of godliness' by receiving priesthood ordinances and making and keeping sacred covenants, we are blessed with strength beyond our own to overcome the temptations and challenges of mortality and to do and become good."[3]

CHAPTER 3

THE HOUSE OF THE LORD: A HOME FOR THE LORD IN OUR DAY

*"We love thy house, O God,
Wherein thine honor dwells.
The joy of thine abode
All earthly joy excels."*

—William Bullock, "We Love Thy House, O God"

My husband and I walked past the Laie Hawaii Temple every day and watched the finishing touches before the open house for its rededication in 2010. We looked through the scaffolding and could see the newly placed words: "Holiness to the Lord, the House of the Lord." We served as tour guides and explained to visitors that as Latter-day Saints we believe in the need for a house of the Lord in a very literal sense. This idea is understandably new for many people. Bringing back this understanding happened gradually in the process of the Restoration.

Why We Need a House of God

From the early days of the Restoration, the Saints received a commandment to build temples. There were times when they seemed to drag their feet, perhaps not fully sure about the temples' purpose or the blessings that would come as a result. This was something new for all of them.

LET'S TALK ABOUT TEMPLES AND RITUAL

First in Kirtland and later in Nauvoo, they labored and sacrificed to build temples, facing opposition at a time when they did not even have chapels in which to worship. They had to dedicate the Nauvoo Temple in stages, starting with the dedication of the baptistry in 1841. It was not until 1846, after the death of Joseph Smith, that the majority of Saints were able to receive their endowment and the temple was fully dedicated. What did they learn along the way that helped them to persevere in fulfilling the Lord's command to build a temple?

By early 1831 the Saints in Fayette, New York, were told something of what the temples were for. The Lord intended that they "might escape the power of the enemy, and be gathered unto me a righteous people, without spot and blameless—Wherefore, for this cause I gave unto you the commandment that ye should go to the Ohio; and there I will give unto you my law; and there you shall be endowed with power from on high" (Doctrine and Covenants 38:31–32). And so, seeking to gather and be more fully empowered, they went to Kirtland, Ohio.

By 1832 in Kirtland, they learned about the priesthood ordinances by which we can enter the presence of the Lord. After an explanation that these blessings received by Abraham, Isaac, and Jacob were not part of the covenant relationship of the Levitical or Aaronic law of Moses, they were told, "And this greater priesthood administereth the gospel and holdeth the key of the mysteries of the kingdom, even the key of the knowledge of God. Therefore, in the ordinances [of this greater Melchizedek Priesthood], the power of godliness is manifest. And without the ordinances thereof, and the authority of the priesthood, the power of godliness is not manifest unto men in the flesh; For without this no man can see the face of God, even the Father, and live" (Doctrine and Covenants 84:19–22).

Through this revelation the early Saints were starting

to get a glimpse of why a house of the Lord needed to be built. The Restoration was going to bring back the covenant blessings—knowledge of God and the power of godliness—that Abraham, Isaac, and Jacob had obtained. This scriptural language, "the knowledge of God" and "the power of godliness," suggests we come to know God because we become like Him. In these temple ordinances, God gives us additional power to be godly and to live a godly life as He does.

Before the Kirtland Temple was completed, the Lord spoke of the glory of His presence, which he wanted to return to the earth through the temples: "And inasmuch as my people build a house unto me in the name of the Lord, and do not suffer any unclean thing to come into it, that it be not defiled, my glory shall rest upon it; Yea, and my presence shall be there, for I will come into it, and all the pure in heart that shall come into it shall see God" (Doctrine and Covenants 97:15–16). The house of the Lord was to be a place where He could be present and where those who were prepared could "see God."

By 1836 the Saints had completed the temple in Kirtland. In the dedicatory prayer, Joseph Smith explained: "For thou knowest that we have done this work through great tribulation; and out of our poverty we have given of our substance to build a house to thy name, that the Son of Man might have a place to manifest himself to his people" (Doctrine and Covenants 109:5). A conviction that the Lord wanted to manifest Himself to His people and that He required a dedicated and sacred place for this encounter gave the early Latter-day Saints strength and vision to sacrifice to receive this blessing. Confidence that what God had to offer was more important than material prosperity and comfort led them to prioritize building the Lord's house. With that same confidence we can likewise sacrifice our time and resources to prioritize spending time in holy temples.

LET'S TALK ABOUT TEMPLES AND RITUAL

Restoration of Needed Keys in Kirtland

After the dedication in 1836, the Lord appeared in the Kirtland Temple to accept it as His house. In His appearance, He confirmed the faith of those who sacrificed so much: "Let the hearts of your brethren rejoice, and let the hearts of all my people rejoice, who have, with their might, built this house to my name. For behold, I have accepted this house, and my name shall be here; and I will manifest myself to my people in mercy in this house. Yea, I will appear unto my servants, and speak unto them with mine own voice, if my people will keep my commandments, and do not pollute this holy house" (Doctrine and Covenants 110:6–8). The new temple was to be a place for the Lord to manifest Himself to all who prepared themselves. The Lord would also restore the additional keys of priesthood authority needed to bring us into the presence of God.

The Saints' effort and sacrifice to build the Kirtland Temple allowed the restoration of certain priesthood keys: keys of the gathering of Israel from Moses, keys of the "dispensation of the gospel of Abraham" from Elias, and keys of the power to "turn the hearts of the fathers to the children, and the children to the fathers" from Elijah (Doctrine and Covenants 110:11–15). The authority of these additional keys enables us to make covenants by participating in temple ordinances, and through these ordinances the knowledge of God and the power of godliness are made available.

Some, like Joseph Smith and Oliver Cowdery, have seen the Risen Lord face-to-face in His house, but for most of us, Christ manifests Himself to us in a way that Nephi described: in the last days "he shall manifest himself unto them in word, and also in power, in very deed, unto the taking away of their stumbling blocks" (1 Nephi 14:1). This is certainly how I have felt Christ manifest Himself to me in the temple. I have found help and healing through my temple worship, and I have seen many stumbling blocks to holiness within myself removed. My desire to seek out the holy increases and my ability to create a sacred place around me is enhanced as I worship in the temple. One way in which I can see my temple service changing me is how much easier it is to keep my house feeling like a temple. Between weekly temple attendance and the years that I served as an ordinance worker, little by little, the peace and order I found in the temple have been increasingly replicated in my home.

For all the spiritual manifestations and restoration of priesthood keys experienced in Kirtland in 1836, the promised covenant blessings were not given until the Saints gathered again in Nauvoo, Illinois. First in the upper room of the Red Brick Store and then in the Nauvoo Temple, Church members were finally able to receive the blessing of the endowment. President Russell M. Nelson explained the contrast between the Kirtland Temple and the one in Nauvoo: "Elijah committed the keys of sealing authority to Joseph Smith in the Kirtland Temple. The fulness of the priesthood was restored in the Nauvoo Temple."[1]

Priesthood keys given in Kirtland were necessary for the administration of temple ordinances. A temple president holds the keys, under which authority all the temple ordinances are performed. Only through the endowment is the "fulness of the priesthood" given to all who come to receive it. The ordinances of the temple make the gift of priesthood power available to all faithful women and men of the Church.

The Fire of the Covenant

Right before they had to journey westward to the Great Basin, the Saints were able to step away from the challenging circumstances of their lives and find solace and strength by seeking the Lord in the temple. Through covenants and ordinances, they were given a spiritual connection to God that provided fortitude and direction to carry on with their journey. They did not escape their problems, but having been given "exceeding great and precious promises,"[2] they were empowered to live in the world with its pain and loss. Having faith in God according to His promises produces the hope we need to keep our hearts oriented toward our true home and spend our lives in God's service.

As they were leaving Nauvoo as refugees, the plight of the poorer Saints became apparent. Brigham Young gave this invitation: "'The poor brethren and sisters, widows and orphans, sick and destitute, are now lying on the west bank of the Mississippi,' he declared. 'Now is the time for labor. Let the fire of the covenant, which you made in the house of the Lord, burn in your hearts, like flame unquenchable.'"[3] The Saints had only just crossed the river and needed power beyond their own to bless and help those in need. It would be a very long and hard journey, but they now had access to divine power through keeping the covenants they had made in the house of the Lord in Nauvoo.

When I was made ward Relief Society president, I printed Brigham Young's statement that "now is the time for labor" and about "the fire of the covenant" and put it under the plastic cover of the binder that held all my papers for my calling. The statement served as a powerful reminder that I was not laboring alone, solely relying on my own strength. Thankfully, because of what I had learned from temple covenants, I knew that I would be able to access divine strength and wisdom to serve as the Lord required. Whenever we start long and hard journeys, we can remember that we have access to a source of divine power because of our covenants. We can know that we will not be alone on our journey.

A HOME FOR THE LORD IN OUR DAY

Promises and God's Faithfulness

We learn in the book of Hebrews that faith in these covenant promises gave the ancient patriarchs and matriarchs power to do what they could not do by themselves:

> By faith Abraham, when he was called to go out into a place which he should after receive for an inheritance, obeyed; and he went out, not knowing whither he went. By faith he sojourned in the land of promise, as in a strange country, dwelling in tabernacles with Isaac and Jacob, the heirs with him of the same promise: For he looked for a city which hath foundations, whose builder and maker is God. Through faith also Sara herself received strength to conceive seed, and was delivered of a child when she was past age, because she judged him faithful who had promised. (Hebrews 11:8–11)

Sarah had faith in the Lord's faithfulness. She miraculously received the covenant blessings because she trusted that God would not lie, that His promises were sure. But Sarah and Abraham also had to wait. These promises were fulfilled in the Lord's time. As these verses suggest, the ultimate covenant inheritance to those who are "heirs with him of the same promise" is something beyond this world. Through covenant we are heirs with the Lord to a celestial inheritance "whose builder and maker is God." God wants to give us all that He has and is; it is in the covenants and ordinances of the temple that those promises are given to us.

As one who has received promises that have not yet been fulfilled in mortality, I have deep appreciation for the confidence Abraham and Sarah displayed, believing in God's promised blessings especially when they remained unfulfilled for a very long time. Having faith in the faithfulness of the One who promised has brought me peace when our efforts to have children and then adopt did not work out as we had hoped. Like Nephi, "I know in whom I have trusted" (2 Nephi 4:19).

God's promises are sure, whether they come to fruition in this life or in the next. The restoration of priesthood ordinances and their associated covenants provides hope that comes from God's certain word, given to us individually by those who are authorized to pronounce those covenant blessings.

Promises on Our Path of Pilgrimage

It can be easy to get disoriented amid the tragedies and tedium of life, but the Lord's covenant promises keep us pointed toward our true destination. The early Saints, like those of ancient days, had confidence in the One who had promised. "These all died in faith, not having received the promises, but having seen them afar off, and were persuaded of them, and embraced them, and confessed that they were strangers and pilgrims on the earth. For they that say such things declare plainly that they seek a country" (Hebrews 11:13–14).

Just as we journey to attend the temple, we are journeying to our eternal home, strengthened by the covenants and ordinances we receive in the temple. We invite all to join us to be gathered in the temple. President Nelson described this as the central focus of our lives and God's plan for us: "The ultimate objective of the gathering of Israel is to bring the blessings of the temple to God's faithful children."[4] We invite all to gather and to individually accept the Savior's invitation: "How oft will I gather you as a hen gathereth her chickens under her wings, if ye will repent and return unto me with full purpose of heart" (3 Nephi 10:6). "He sendeth an invitation unto all men, for the arms of mercy are extended towards them, and he saith: Repent, and I will receive you" (Alma 5:33).

Heavenly Father invites all His children home, and through the blessings of Christ's atoning sacrifice made available in the temple, He is preparing us to be there with Him. In the words of BYU religion professor Brad Wilcox, "The miracle of the Atonement is not just that we can go home but that—miraculously—we can feel at home there."[5] As we next consider how temple ritual orients us to God, we can begin to more fully appreciate how we come unto Christ and partake of the fruit of His atoning sacrifice in the sacred time and space of the temple.

CHAPTER 4

RITUAL ORIENTATION: SACRED TIME AND SPACE

> *"Prone to wander, Lord, I feel it*
> *Prone to leave the God I love;*
> *Here's my heart, O take and seal it;*
> *Seal it for thy courts above."*
>
> —Robert Robinson, "Come,
>   Thou Fount of Every Blessing"

Elder Jeffrey R. Holland has challenged us: "When one goes to the holy temple for the first time, he or she may be somewhat awestruck by that experience. Our job is to ensure that the sacred symbols and revealed rituals, the ceremonial clothing and visual presentations, never distract from but rather point toward the Savior, whom we are there to worship."[1]

Temple rituals are different from what we experience in our Sunday worship. Sometimes we might wonder why and what we are supposed to learn from them. Other questions that can be helpful to ask are "What is ritual?" and "How is learning from ritual different from learning from a talk or a lecture?" I hope that by exploring the orienting power of sacred rituals in the temple, we can more fully recognize the Savior and His invitation to come unto Him.

RITUAL ORIENTATION: SACRED TIME AND SPACE

Worship and Becoming

As we think about temple ritual and worship, it helps to remember that, even in a modern and secular world, everyone worships something. We are all shaped and changed by our worship, even if we don't realize what direction that change is taking us. We are moving from one way of being to another. We are all on journeys. By choosing to participate in temple ritual and temple worship, we are choosing to change what we are becoming.

We all seek out what we love. Our lives are a quest to become and achieve what we value and treasure. Amid a wide variety of choices and options presented by our culture and context, we all orient ourselves to what matters in the world. We all choose what path to follow and what to pursue. The experiences and activities we choose then orient us and shape our values and priorities. Making temple worship a part of our regular lives helps to orient and shape everything that we do outside of the temple.

Ritual as Orientation

Let me start by giving an analogy. I'm a bird-watcher. My husband and I love to be outside in nature. When we lived in Hawaii, we were excited every fall to see the plovers return from summering in Alaska. They would fly thousands of miles nonstop to return to the exact location from which they left. Birds have extraordinary senses that orient them to the world. Many of them annually make a journey of great distances. They have a sense of time and space that helps them know when and where to go.

As humans in a modern and secular world, we have lost many of the sources of orientation that give us a sense of time and space related to our heavenly home. Answers to the deep questions of the soul regarding who we are, where we should be going, and who we can become are part of what the Restoration of Christ's Church offers. The Lord wants to orient us on our journey of life and help us return to Him. In the temple we are shown how we fit into the story of the plan of redemption, which was prepared before the foundation of the world. We are offered direction and power to return home.

This orienting message in the temple is, however, expressed in ritual space, time, action, and clothing that belongs to a more ancient world. Elder David A. Bednar observed, "Gospel covenants and ordinances operate in our lives much like a compass. A compass is a device used to indicate the cardinal directions of north, south, east, and west for purposes of navigation and geographic orientation. In a similar way, our covenants and ordinances point us to and help us always remember our connection with the Lord Jesus Christ as we progress along the covenant path."[2] As we come to know God more fully by participating in the ordinances of the temple and then living out the covenants associated with them, we come to know Christ as the way home and receive His power to get there.

Ritual and Religious Practice

In the modern world, we often think about religion in terms of belief, but religious *practice*, what people do, is perhaps far more important. We can understand more about temple ritual from our friends of other faiths and their religious practices. My husband and I both studied religion in our PhD programs at Claremont Graduate University in eastern Los Angeles County. One Saturday morning when Keith was in a class on Judaism, we joined a class outing and traveled to downtown LA to attend Jewish Sabbath services. We had often seen devout Orthodox families walking to their synagogues as we drove to the LA temple on Friday nights and Saturdays, but this Saturday, with Keith's class, we had a chance to enter several of those synagogues ourselves.

Even though the temple in Jerusalem was destroyed in

RITUAL ORIENTATION: SACRED TIME AND SPACE

AD 70, Jews have sought to keep their worship alive without having a temple in their midst. However, in recent centuries, there have been divisions within Judaism about how a life of worship and devotion should be practiced. That morning we attended several services: one in a small Orthodox synagogue, where the men and women heard and read scripture texts separated by a divider; one in a Conservative synagogue where we sat in a large auditorium together and looked at the rabbi, who was on a stage; and one with a small, liberal gathering where everyone sat and learned together.

Simply by choosing to gather and to worship, all these believers were *oriented* to live in the world differently than others around them. They saw themselves as Jewish and had a desire to escape the pull of modern culture and values through the symbolic action of Sabbath worship, which directed them to something beyond the present. Like them, we can choose to participate in religious ritual in the temple, which allows us to step away from the world and its contemporary values and starts us on a pathway of discipleship.

Another thing I saw was how discipleship is a practice of *embodiment*—participants in each of these different traditions of Judaism dressed and met together differently. They each embodied their distinct interpretation of scripture with their worship practices. I saw up close this range of practice, from traditional to modern. Just as some of the ways in which we as Latter-day Saints worship are different from contemporary norms, many other forms of religious worship do not feel the need to adapt to modern sensibilities.

Religious rituals function as a map or compass to guide people's choices and keep them oriented to the path they are choosing to follow. In more contemporary forms of Judaism, participants' lives are much like other modern people's. By contrast, the ancient temple's ritual distinction between clean

LET'S TALK ABOUT TEMPLES AND RITUAL

and unclean, sacred and profane, is particularly clear in the practice of Orthodox Judaism.

Orientation to time is one way religious ritual allows believers to experience the sacred. For instance, Orthodox Jews' careful observance of the Sabbath as a sacred day in which they do no work focuses them weekly and reminds them to prioritize God in their lives. This is a practice Latter-day Saints can identify with since the commandment to keep the Sabbath day holy is one we also strive to live. Ritual regarding food is another way to stay oriented. It takes a great deal of effort to keep the dietary laws of Orthodox Judaism, and the Jews who choose to keep kosher practice that ritual daily, distinguishing holy from unholy. When we as Latter-day Saints keep our covenants and remain worthy to enter the temple by keeping the Word of Wisdom and the law of chastity, we find similar opportunities to separate ourselves from worldliness and to seek lives of holiness that put God first.

Place is another facet of religious practice and ritual that can shape the faithful's experience of the world. Growing up in the Washington, DC, suburbs, I had a chance to visit the Islamic Center of Washington and came to appreciate the members' orientation to sacred space. As I entered the Islamic Center, I removed my shoes. I saw how Muslims bow down and worship together as they pray facing Mecca.

Visiting Jerusalem as an adult, I saw special markings on the door celebrating those Muslims who made the pilgrimage to Mecca (the hajj). Mecca is sacred within Islam, and non-Muslims are not allowed into the city, but I have seen recordings of how, as part of the hajj, all involved dress in simple white garments and follow in the footsteps of Mohammed. By being in that sacred place, Muslims participate in sacred history, seeking to more fully submit to God, as did their exemplar. As Latter-day Saints worshipping in the temple, we have a similar experience of dressing in white to participate in sacred history through the presentation of the endowment.

I feel a deep sense of kinship with worshippers of many faiths who, through participation in religious action, experience a shared identity and purpose. Often this identity and purpose are expressed through clothing, orienting the wearer toward the sacred in daily life. Just as we wear the temple garment as a constant reminder of the covenants we have made, Orthodox Jewish men always keep their head covered by wearing a kippah or yarmulke. Many Muslim women stay oriented to God by wearing a head covering or hijab. Those who are ministers, priests, or nuns likewise have clothing, such as clerical colors, head coverings, or robes, by which they can be recognized.

By orienting toward and identifying with something beyond the pull of secular culture, we can tune our hearts to the love of God. In the practices of worship we become worshipful; in the practices of devotion we become devout. By practicing these holy rituals and sacred rites, we become our true selves. We become connected and aligned with God.

Liturgy and Worship

Growing up, we didn't call our meetings at church a "worship service." As I witnessed other traditions, our Sunday worship services seemed rather ordinary compared to those who have elaborate liturgical practices ("liturgy" refers to the sequence of rituals of a worship service). Our Sunday meetings are similar to the meetings of many Protestants. No one wears special clothing other than "Sunday best." The blessing and passing of the sacrament is a simple practice. We all share our thoughts and faith in talks given from the pulpit.

When I went to the mass for the marriage of our beloved babysitter and neighbor, my young eyes were opened to an elaborate liturgy, a sequence of ritual practices. These practices included special clothing, or "vestments," worn by priests; processions; incense; kneeling; and other actions. The surprise I felt then is often felt by Latter-day Saints who attend the temple for the first time and realize temple liturgy is unlike anything they may have experienced before.

Unlike during Sunday worship services, everyone in the temple wears special ritual clothing. The Church website explains: "Temple robes of The Church of Jesus Christ of Latter-day Saints, known as the robes of the holy priesthood, are worn only inside Latter-day Saint temples and reserved for the most sacred ceremonies of their faith. Simple white clothing symbolizes purity and equality. The most senior Church leader and the newest member are indistinguishable when dressed in the same way. Men and women wear similar clothing, which evokes religious symbolism reminiscent of temple practices described in the Old Testament."[3]

The clothing and other ritual elements of temple ordinances are elaborate and filled with symbolism. It can certainly seem like a surprising contrast to our Sunday worship. The first part of the endowment, known as the initiatory ordinance, is sometimes also called the washing and anointing. This ordinance is administered individually, helped by temple ordinance workers. These "ordinances include special blessings regarding [our] divine heritage and potential. As part of these ordinances," we are also "authorized to wear the sacred temple garment."[4] (The symbolism of the temple garment is explored more fully in chapter six.)

The second part of the endowment takes place as part of a group in which men and women receive instruction and make covenants. "Events that are part [of] the plan of salvation are presented. They include the Creation of the world, the Fall of Adam and Eve, the Atonement of Jesus Christ, the Apostasy, and the Restoration." Participants "also learn more about the way all people can return to the presence of the Lord. Some of the endowment is presented through video and some by temple officiators."[5]

This part of the endowment includes symbolic movement and progression, which sometimes involves moving from room to room, depending on the layout of the temple. We feel a unity in being the Lord's people and dedicating ourselves to Him. Together we symbolically experience returning to the presence of God as we finish the ordinance and then enter into the celestial room to be with our family or to ponder, pray, and read scriptures.

Like ritual action in many faiths, the ritual action of the endowment requires knowing what to do and how to do it. Mastering all the details can take time to learn, but in the temple, there is always someone there to help at every stage of the learning process. There is no need to learn it all the first time. In my service as a temple worker, helping newer patrons was a very special opportunity, and I was always very grateful to be there to provide support.

Like the liturgy of Catholic mass, with its sequence of prayers, readings, kneeling, and processions, the liturgy of temple worship is an order of rituals we participate in, and it's something we learn over time. As we participate in temple liturgy, we orient ourselves to how we should live and what is important. Through participation in this series of ritual actions, we are given a narrative of who we are and what matters in life. Our worship shapes us and changes us.

Ritual Knowledge in the Old Testament

Coming from a modern world that thinks about information as facts one is given, we may at first find that the symbolic language of the temple feels unfamiliar. Through temple ritual we are taught about Christ's Atonement, how to live, and how to return home, but it is a different way of learning. In Hebrew the verb for knowing (*yada*) focuses on knowing by experience rather than just knowing facts. It emphasizes being in a relationship with God. Knowing the Lord is a way of walking faithfully within the covenant with God. Ritual is a way in which we can gain knowledge by lived experience rather than just being given information.

Faithful participation in the practices of the law of Moses gave the Israelites the opportunity to experience a knowledge of God through repentance and sacrifice. By contrast, the Bible describes those who do not worship and obey as those who do not know God (see Hosea 4:1–2, 6). The verbs translated as "worship" in the King James Version focus on *practice*, what we do with our bodies rather than just what we believe. These Hebrew terms are "bow down" (*ḥwh*) and "serve" (*ābad*).

The message I take from the Old Testament is that as we worship, bowing down and serving, we come to know God in an embodied sense. Rather than simply having more information about God, we learn to follow His model and start to take on His way of being. Christ taught that eternal life is knowing Him and His Father (John 17:3). King Benjamin asked, "How knoweth a man the master whom he has not served, and who is a stranger unto him, and is far from the thoughts and intents of his heart?" (Mosiah 5:13). We come to know Him as our God through our temple service. In the ritual actions of our worship, we orient ourselves to Him and His will, and we prepare ourselves to go home and do His will.

Seeking God and Tasting the Fruit

We can see the need to stay oriented to our destination in the story of Lehi's dream. Like the presentation of the endowment in the temple, this story is a model for the journey we are making back to God. Lehi's dream demonstrates how ritual works and how knowledge comes through participation. Lehi saw a tree that he could tell was special and moved toward that destination. When he arrived, Lehi partook of the fruit and came to know the love of God.

Elder David A. Bednar taught, "The fruit on the tree is a symbol for the blessings of [Jesus Christ's] Atonement. Partaking of the fruit of the tree represents the receiving of ordinances and covenants whereby the Atonement can become fully efficacious in our lives."[6] Just like the knowledge that we gain through the ordinances and covenants of the temple, the knowledge Lehi gained didn't come from being told about the love of God. He experienced it. He participated and took it into Himself as he partook of the fruit of the tree. He knew by lived experience how delicious it was. Each choice we make to come closer to Christ, to follow promptings of the Holy Ghost, and especially to make and keep covenants allows us to partake of that fruit.

The story of Lehi's spiritual journey helps us understand the spiritual journey that we must make to have our own encounter with the love of God. Likewise, the presentation of the temple endowment helps us see our lives in terms of this journey back to the presence of God. Elder Neil L. Andersen taught, "Partaking of the fruit of the tree also symbolizes that we embrace the ordinances and covenants of the restored gospel—being baptized, receiving the gift of the Holy Ghost, and entering the house of the Lord to be endowed with power from on high."[7] As we come to see and feel the Lord's love in the ordinances of the temple, we can more fully commit to staying on the covenant path in our daily lives.

I have my own experience of coming to taste that fruit, which prepared me to seek for greater light and knowledge in the temple. I was nineteen years old when my sister and I had a chance to travel in Europe for much of the summer. We were living up to the light and knowledge that we had, making sure to keep our covenants and seeking out Church meetings wherever we happened to be each Sunday. In city after city, we had a wonderful time making connections between what we saw and what we had studied in our European and art history classes. At church one Sunday in Brussels, we "happened" to run into our former stake president and his wife, President and Sister Rouché, who were serving as mission leaders there. They invited us to the mission office for a tour and then to the mission home for dinner.

I can honestly say that up to that point I had "been myself a follower of righteousness, desiring also to be one who possessed great knowledge" (Abraham 1:2), but I thought I would find the knowledge that I was seeking with my mind and reason. Something President Rouché said when we were in the mission home forever changed my view on this topic. When he pointed out the room where the new missionaries stayed, he explained that after the first night at the mission home, he had them meet their trainers and then sent them off. With my inquiring and analytical mind, I asked how he decided who would serve as trainers. I assumed there would be certain criteria that he weighed out. Instead, he said simply, "Revelation."

It was as though another dimension of reality opened up, and I realized that I knew nothing about it. It was new territory, a world that I was not living in. What I felt while talking with him and being in the mission home and office changed my heart as well as my mind. I didn't know exactly what I was feeling, but more than anything I wanted to be a missionary so I could keep that feeling. Returning to school at BYU that fall semester, I started to prepare to receive my endowment before my mission the next year.

I studied the Book of Mormon every day, and the desire to partake of the fruit of the tree kept growing within me, helping me have courage to make changes in my life. I could picture myself wearing the garment and receiving additional spiritual power. I could almost feel the fabric end right above my knee. I wanted to receive that endowment more than anything, and I oriented my life around that priority, making course corrections and taking on new ways of doing things. Even after a lifetime of faithful membership in the Church, what I felt that summer in Brussels gave me a taste of the fruit of the tree. It was delicious, and I wanted to keep journeying to partake more fully.

As I felt the increased desire to seek after God, I received additional direction to keep me walking in the right direction, to move toward the tree with its precious fruit. I remembered President Ezra Taft Benson's then-recent promise that when you put the Lord first, everything will fall into place or fall out of your life.[8] Choosing to trust that promise and follow the promptings that came, I became more careful in my religious practices. This served to reorient and reshape my life. The choice to live with attention to God's commandments prepares us for the temple because it is precisely this orientation to put God first that temple worship reinforces and embodies.

Seeking God and Temple Blessings

Abraham is known as the father of the faithful in many religious traditions because of his fixed love for God that kept him on the path. He knew what he wanted was to draw close to God, and he oriented his life accordingly. We read in the book of Abraham that he saw through the sham of false worship and values of his contemporary society and realized that he needed to seek out God elsewhere. "In the land of the Chaldeans, at the residence of my fathers, I, Abraham, saw that it was needful for me to obtain another place of residence." He could tell that what and how people around him were worshipping was a false substitute for true worship of the true God. He explained: "finding there was greater happiness and peace and rest for me, I sought for the blessings of the fathers, and the right whereunto I should be ordained to administer the same" (Abraham 1:1–2).

LET'S TALK ABOUT TEMPLES AND RITUAL

We all seek happiness. What is amazing about Abraham is that he recognized this search was connected with the priesthood blessings of the temple. Seeking for "greater happiness and peace and rest," he "sought for the blessings of the fathers, and the right whereunto [he] should be ordained to administer the same" (Abraham 1:2). In other words, Abraham sought revealed ritual and ordinance. He was good but knew that he needed help and power to be better and to more fully know God. He continued, "Having been myself a follower of righteousness, desiring also to be one who possessed great knowledge, and to be a greater follower of righteousness, and to possess a greater knowledge, and to be a father of many nations, a prince of peace, and desiring to receive instructions, and to keep the commandments of God, I became a rightful heir, a High Priest, holding the right belonging to the fathers" (Abraham 1:2).

President Benson corrected the idea that this scriptural text is about wanting to be ordained to a priesthood office but is instead about the priesthood blessings offered to all in the temple. He observed that "because of its sacredness we are sometimes reluctant to say anything about the temple to our children and grandchildren. As a consequence, many do not develop a real desire to go to the temple, or when they go there, they do so without much background to prepare them for the obligations and covenants they enter into." He further explained: "I believe a proper understanding or background will immeasurably help prepare our youth for the temple. This understanding, I believe, will foster within them a desire to seek their priesthood blessings just as Abraham sought his."[9]

When we know that the temple is where we all, both women and men, receive our priesthood blessings, we can be like Abraham, seeking priesthood blessings, what we refer to as the endowment and the sealing. The priesthood blessings that he received through making and keeping covenants were the template for the blessings that the Lord has restored in our day.

Even if we can no more than *desire* to believe or simply *want* to want something better, it is enough. Choosing to seek out God as He reveals Himself in His temple enables Him to change our hearts. As we learn to worship, bowing down and serving, we allow Him to reveal Himself to us. His promise is that as we seek Him, we too can possess greater knowledge and experience His way of being. In the rituals of the temple, we are connected to the knowledge of "the only true God, and Jesus Christ, whom [He has] sent" (John 17:3). As we participate in the ordinance of the endowment, we practice holiness, taking on the name and nature of the Holy One of Israel. Rather than just giving us information, the temple allows us to become more fully converted, which, in President Dallin H. Oaks's words "requires us to do and to become."[10]

Ritual and Discipleship

Worship in the temple helps us learn to worship God above anything else. That orientation to God is then lived out in regular practices of discipleship. We use our time differently when we pray and study scriptures first thing each day. We relate to consumer culture differently when we pay our tithing first each payday. Our bodies and social relationships are different when we keep the Word of Wisdom and law of chastity. Through lives of discipleship we are changed and converted. "We are challenged to move through a process of conversion toward that status and condition called eternal life."[11] This is the journey and pilgrimage of a disciple. We seek to be where God is as we seek to become as He is.

The temple has insightfully been called the Lord's university. Here, where the Lord is, we can be tutored in a godly way of walking in the world. President Oaks explained, "The gospel of Jesus Christ is the plan by which we can become what children of God are supposed to become. This spotless and perfected state will result from a steady succession of covenants, ordinances, and actions, an accumulation of right choices, and from continuing repentance."[12] We need tutoring and practice to learn how to walk in the world without becoming worldly. In the sacred space and time that the temple offers, we symbolically step out of the world for a moment so that we can return to live in the world in a holy way, walking with God, having Christ's name more fully upon us.

CHAPTER 5

THE JOURNEY: CONTINUING ON THE COVENANT PATH

*"We love thee, Lord; our hearts are full.
We'll walk thy chosen way."*
—Lee Tom Perry, "As Now We Take the Sacrament"

Years ago, during some professional meetings, I ate dinner with a kindly older Lutheran minister and professor. He took the opportunity to ask me some questions about Latter-day Saint beliefs he had heard about that seemed unusual to him. I particularly remember that he was troubled with the idea that we do temple "work." For those in a Lutheran tradition, this focus on "work" seems antithetical to the good news of the gospel that we are saved through Christ and not our own works.

For some of those not of our faith, and for some Latter-day Saints as well, part of the perceived disconnect between the temple and the doctrine of Christ stems from a lack of understanding, an inability to see the link between the idea of becoming like God and the gospel message. Without really appreciating the good news of the gospel—that salvation is only in and through Christ—we might see the temple as a place where we go to do work to save ourselves. Missing the role of Christ, we might think we need to arrive back at our heavenly home and become like God on our own. Without seeing the role of Christ as our Redeemer, the journey can feel overwhelming.

But as we come to see the temple as the continuation of the covenant path that connects us to our Redeemer, we see the clarity and unity of the plan of redemption. In this chapter I will explore how in the ordinances of the temple we see the gift of His atoning power and exercise our agency in choosing to receive that gift.

The Covenant Path

In his groundbreaking first address after becoming prophet, President Russell M. Nelson issued an invitation: "To each member of the Church I say, keep on the covenant path. Your commitment to follow the Savior by making covenants with Him and then keeping those covenants will open the door to every spiritual blessing and privilege available to men, women, and children everywhere."[1]

Anciently the children of Israel were told: "You must follow exactly the path that the Lord your God has commanded you, so that you may live, and that it may go well with you, and that you may live long in the land that you are to possess" (Deuteronomy 5:33, NRSV). When Christ came, He testified, "I am the way, the truth, and the life: no man cometh unto the Father, but by me" (John 14:6). In Christ we are given the way to follow the path.

Following the covenant path does not mean that we never make a mistake. Instead, the path is how we are redeemed, how with Christ's help we learn to walk in His way. We are shown how and empowered to take on His name and nature through the temple covenants and in the ordinances.

Eternal life is a *way* of being, and so we cannot receive it unless we participate in this way of being. Learning to come unto the Father through Christ is the journey of the covenant path. It is the journey of the temple.

Because we are not perfect, as we follow the path, Christ offers us a way to return to it when needed, a way to change course, to repent. Christ was "lifted up upon the cross and slain for the sins of the world" (1 Nephi 11:33). The ordinances of salvation connect us with Christ's sacrifice for our redemption. "And my Father sent me that I might be lifted up upon the cross; and after that I had been lifted up upon the cross, that I might draw all men unto me" (3 Nephi 27:14). Through the covenants and ordinances of the temple, we can receive the gift of His atoning sacrifice and thus be drawn closer and closer to Him.

Discipleship

Mountains functioned as temples in the Old Testament, and, similarly, to give the Sermon on the Mount, Christ left the multitudes and "went up into a mountain: and when he was set, his disciples came unto him" (Matthew 5:1). The term *disciple* is more clearly translated from the Greek *mathetes* as "pupil," "learner," or "apprentice." The disciples were the ones who climbed the mountain to learn of the Lord and to receive His law. In the Melchizedek Priesthood ordinances of the temple, just as in the Aaronic Priesthood ordinances of baptism and the sacrament, we present ourselves to the Lord as His apprentices, willing to learn from our Master. Our desire, our willingness to learn and change our way of being, determines how much He can teach us and help us on that journey.

Christ gives us the gift of the Holy Ghost through the ordinance of confirmation, but we must daily choose to receive it. We are offered the tokens of Christ's atoning sacrifice each week in the sacrament, but we must choose to receive them. In the unfolding of the covenant path in the endowment ceremony, we are repeatedly given gifts of power and love that we must choose to receive, step-by-step, as we progress toward God's presence.

These gifts in temple ordinances are given so "that they may grow up in [Him], and receive a fulness of the Holy Ghost, and be organized according to [His] laws, and be prepared to obtain every needful thing" (Doctrine and Covenant 109:15).[2] The Lord wants to give us power to do and become all that we have covenanted to do and become.

"An Embodiment or an Unfolding"

President Harold B. Lee taught that the endowment expands what we started in baptism: "The receiving of the endowment requires the assuming of obligations by covenants which in reality are but an embodiment or an unfolding of the covenants each person should have assumed at baptism."[3] The phrase that he used, "an embodiment or an unfolding," explains how the ritual action of the temple allow us to enact and embody a life that is changed through receiving Christ.

The endowment "unpacks" and unfolds the symbolically rich message of baptism. In the ritual action of baptism, Christ humbled Himself before the Father and witnessed unto the Father His willingness to live a life of obedience by His embodied immersion in the water. He ritually submitted His own will to the will of the Father. Just as His will was to be swallowed up in the will of the Father, He was swallowed up in the waters of baptism. In the rituals of the temple, our symbolic action likewise indicates our willingness to do and become like Christ.

In the ordinances, we ritually experience coming out of the world and being redeemed through Christ. In baptism we embody Christ. We ritually die, are buried, and rise again with Him. We also covenant to be obedient as He did in His baptism (see 2 Nephi 31:7, 10). In response to this willingness, we are given the gift of the Holy Ghost to give us power to do and become what we have promised. This pattern continues in the gradual, step-by-step process of the endowment.

CONTINUING ON THE COVENANT PATH

Learning as We Go

The ordinance of baptism is offered to those who are "*desirous* to come into the fold of God, and to be called his people, and are *willing* to bear one another's burdens, that they may be light" (Mosiah 18:8; emphasis added). Our willingness to serve and obey manifests our desire to be his people, to take His name and nature upon us. Likewise, temple ordinances give us the name and power of Christ to *do* and *be* what we could never do and be on our own, if that is what we want.

In the endowment ceremony, as we participate in the ordinances, we make covenants to live in a godlier way. These covenants, as outlined in the Church's *General Handbook*, are as follows:

- Live the law of obedience and strive to keep Heavenly Father's commandments.
- Obey the law of sacrifice, which means sacrificing to support the Lord's work and repenting with a broken heart and contrite spirit.
- Obey the law of the gospel of Jesus Christ, which is the higher law that He taught while He was on the earth.
- Keep the law of chastity, which means that a member has sexual relations only with the person to whom he or she is legally and lawfully wedded according to God's law.
- Keep the law of consecration, which means that members dedicate their time, talents, and everything with which the Lord has blessed them to building up Jesus Christ's Church on the earth.[4]

As we make covenants in the ordinance of the endowment, we pledge ourselves to be holy. We make promises about the kind of life we will live. By doing, so we indicate that we *want* to take upon us the name and nature of Christ.

While our covenant promises bind us to holiness, it is critical to remember that "the word endowment means 'a gift.' In this context, the temple endowment is a gift of sacred blessings from God to each of us. . . . Some of the gifts you receive through the temple endowment include:

1. Greater knowledge of the Lord's purposes and teachings.
2. Power to do all that God wants us to do.
3. Divine guidance and protection as we serve the Lord, our families, and others.
4. Increased hope, comfort, and peace.
5. Promised blessings now and forever."[5]

Christ offers us these gifts through the ordinance of the endowment, and we use our faith to choose to receive them.

Though we ritually experience the giving and reception of gifts in the ordinances, we only fully receive these gifts of the Savior's atoning power when we *want* to do His will and go forth to keep our covenants. Our desire to do His will as His disciples leads us to obey and helps us to *receive* the gifts He wants to give us.

Willingness

English has its roots in German, and the verb *willen*, "to want or desire," appears often in scripture. "Whosoever *will* come may come and partake of the waters of life freely; and whosoever *will not* come the same is not compelled to come" (Alma 42:27; emphasis added). We receive what we are *willing* to receive (see Doctrine and Covenants 88:32). We offer our *will* to the Lord (see Luke 22:42).

Sometimes, recognizing our weakness, we hesitate to make additional commitments to the Lord; this can be a stumbling block keeping us from going to the temple and receiving our endowment. President Lee reassured us: "Any [people] who [are] prepared to assume those obligations declared by Alma and 'who humble themselves before God . . . and come forth with broken hearts and contrite spirits . . . and are *willing to take upon them the name of Jesus Christ, having a determination to serve him to the end' (D&C 20:37), need have no hesitancy in going to a holy temple* and receiving, in connection with the covenants taken, promises of great blessings predicated upon compliance therewith."[6] We covenant that we will obey, but we are also given additional power to obey through our participation in the ordinances.

The good news of the gospel is that, if we want to be better and different, the Lord can work with us. If that is what we want to do and be, then we will be given the capacity to do and be that. As we return to worship and serve in the temple, we feel a renewal of power. The message conveyed in temple ordinances is that Christ's cleansing and enabling power is offered to us as we make and keep covenants.

I felt that strengthening help at a time in my life when I was turning my wheels. A year after we moved to Laie to teach at BYU–Hawaii, Keith was called as a bishop of a student ward. The evenings when he was gone to attend meetings, I would often sit and watch television just to have some company. One evening, I felt a desire for something more, something better than another episode of *Entertainment Tonight*, and I walked up the hill to the temple five minutes from my house to do initiatory work.

That choice was a turning point for me. I knew I needed help in so many areas of my life, but choosing to go to the temple that night and every "bishop night" after was how I chose to learn of Christ rather than the world. Christ was there in the temple, waiting to give me help I needed, but I had to be willing to turn away from the world and make the climb to find Him there.

Continuing on the Path

If we are willing, God can work with us. As we make temple covenants in the ordinance of the endowment, we also receive gifts that enable us to take on Christ's nature of obedience, sacrifice, chastity, and consecration. If we want to be obedient, if we want to sacrifice, if we want to be chaste and consecrate ourselves to God, God can work with us. When we say yes to God, we receive His power. When we say yes to God, we give Him permission to work in our lives to change our nature. The enabling and empowering gifts He wants to give us depend upon our willingness to receive.

On those days when we don't want what God wants as much as we would like, choosing to participate in the ordinances with "real intent," at least wanting to want something different, helps us embody and inhabit willingness (see 2 Nephi 31:13). By ritually embodying Christ's willingness, we can reset our hearts to more fully want what God wants. We use our agency to open our hearts to be changed by His Spirit.

The process of wanting what the Lord wants and aligning our will with His is a long journey. Regular temple worship helps us in this process of "putt[ing] off the natural man and becom[ing] a saint through the atonement of Christ the Lord" (Mosiah 3:19). At times, when a spiritual prompting comes, I don't follow up as quickly as I should. I have found that the more I serve in the temple, the quicker I am to listen and obey.

In the temple we ritually immerse ourselves in a life of obedience. We practice holiness. In this way, our hearts can be reset, over and over again, to want what God wants and to walk His chosen way. In the words of Elder Jeffrey R. Holland, "If you are endowed, go to the temple as often as your circumstances allow. Remember that the temple arms you 'with [God's] power, . . . [puts His] glory . . . round about [you], and [gives His] angels . . . charge over [you].' And when you leave the temple, remember the symbols you take with you, never to be set aside or forgotten."[7]

CHAPTER 6

NEW IDENTITY: PUTTING ON CHRIST

"What can I give him, poor as I am?
If I were a shepherd, I would bring a lamb;
If I were a wise man, I would do my part;
Yet what can I give him? Give him my heart."
—Christina Rossetti, "In the Bleak Midwinter"

The idea of wearing ceremonial clothing for special occasions isn't too hard to understand. Putting clothing on and off is part of how we put an identity on and off. Throughout the world there are special occasions that we dress up for, either for cultural or religious purposes. Even if we don't like "dressing up" for fancy occasions, we might feel it's okay to dress up to ritually play a role in a ceremony or special event, such as a wedding, funeral, party, or graduation. In the modern world we tend to be grateful when the special occasion is over, glad for the return to informality and the opportunity to take off the ritual clothing and get back to "being ourselves."

But what if we were not supposed to put off our new self, with our new name and covenant identity? The Church has stated, "As part of entering into these covenants in the temple, members receive a simple undergarment—often referred to as the 'temple garment' or 'garment of the Holy Priesthood.' Unlike other ceremonial clothing used during the endowment, the garment is worn underneath members' normal clothing for the rest of their lives, serving as a daily physical reminder of their covenant relationship with God."[1]

For some, the requirement of wearing the garment of the Holy Priesthood, given as part of the endowment, may be a source of confusion or frustration for various reasons. In a modern world in which self-expression and personal comfort are highly prized, the expectation to wear the temple garment day and night could be challenging.

As we understand the endowment, we come to realize that our covenant identity and name are manifest in daily practices of what we wear. As we choose to wear the garment of the Holy Priesthood day and night, we are fulfilling what the Lord told Moses: "ye shall be unto me a kingdom of priests [and priestesses], and an holy nation" (Exodus 19:6). I saw this covenant faithfulness modeled by my devoted parents, who wore their temple garments under knee-length shorts in the stifling heat and humidity of Virginia summers. They might have found excuses to remove the garment, but they didn't.

Baptized into His Death

The meaning and purpose of wearing the temple garment may best be addressed by exploring how, with the garment of the Holy Priesthood, we "put on Christ" as part of our covenant relationship with Him. A fuller sense of how we ritually embody Christ's atoning sacrifice, and thus "put on Christ" through making temple covenants, can be found in scriptures that explain baptism.

Paul referred to the radical change that covenants make possible, and he used the language of clothing to communicate his point: "For as many of you as have been baptized into Christ have put on Christ" (Galatians 3:27). How do we "put on" Christ through temple ordinances? Paul developed this idea more fully in Romans by pointing to the ritual identification with Christ that comes with the ordinances: "Know ye

NEW IDENTITY: PUTTING ON CHRIST

not, that so many of us as were baptized into Jesus Christ were baptized into his death?" (Romans 6:3). We ritually experience His death and burial in the ordinances.

After a lifetime of always doing the Father's will, Christ gave up his life, fully expressing His humility and submission to the Father. His death was also the source of new life, eternal life for Him and for us. "Therefore we are buried with him by baptism into death: that like as Christ was raised up from the dead by the glory of the Father, even so we also should walk in newness of life" (Romans 6:4). After ritually participating in the death and burial of Christ through baptism, we ritually rise with Christ. As in baptism, in the ordinances of the temple, we ritually experience Christ's atoning sacrifice and Crucifixion through symbolic actions and then ritually enter into newness of life in the celestial kingdom.

In our ritual submission and resurrection with Christ through the ordinances, we begin to walk in a new way with a new identity, having taken His name upon us. It's a way of walking that requires a lifetime of practice and repeated, even daily, repentance to keep learning and becoming what we have promised (and been promised) to become. Our discipleship is an apprenticeship in putting on Christ, practicing taking on a new way of being in the world. In the temple we are ritually clothed with the robes of the Holy Priesthood. In our temple worship we learn to embody a new name and identity as a perfectly obedient child of God, even as Christ is. After leaving the temple, we are daily reminded to put on Christ as we put on the holy garment that points to Him.

Newness of Life

Through the ordinances we are promised and ritually experience redemption and salvation so we can enjoy a freedom from sin the rest of our lives, walking in the newness of life we are given. In teaching about baptism, Paul explained the larger pattern of ritual participation in temple ordinances that orients us toward a new life in Christ: "For if we have been planted together in the likeness of his death, we shall be also in the likeness of his resurrection" (Romans 6:5). By embodying Christ in the ordinances, we experience both the submission of death and the exalting power that lifts us to a holier form of life.

Just as with baptism, when we participate in the temple ordinances, we move forward having received the promise of a glorious resurrection and a life with Christ. "Knowing this, that our old man is crucified with him, that the body of sin might be destroyed, that henceforth we should not serve sin" (Romans 6:6). In other words, the pattern that we experience in the ordinances of salvation is this: by ritually embodying Christ's death, He redeems us, and we emerge to serve Him rather than serving sin. But even though we covenant to serve God in the temple ordinances, learning to serve God rather than sin requires a lifetime of practice.

By regularly participating in temple ordinances, our actions, hearts, and minds can gradually change. Elder David A. Bednar taught, "Our hearts—the sum total of our desires, affections, intentions, motives, and attitudes—define who we are and determine what we will become. And the essence of the Lord's work is changing, turning, and purifying hearts through gospel covenants and priesthood ordinances."[2] The Lord gives us the covenants and ordinances to help us have this change of heart, to more fully put off the natural man and become saints through the Atonement of Christ (see Mosiah 3:19).

As we participate in temple ordinances, our sinful life ritually dies with Christ, and we emerge victorious through Him, empowered by covenant to live unto God. "Now if we be dead with Christ, we believe that we shall also live with him: Knowing that Christ being raised from the dead dieth no more; death hath no more dominion over him. For in that he died, he died unto sin once: but in that he liveth, he liveth unto God" (Romans 6:8–10). Going forth from the temple, as we wear the temple garment, we remember that we have been redeemed from sin and are living unto God. "The garment provides a constant reminder of the covenants made in the temple. . . . When worn properly, the garment provides protection against temptation and evil. Wearing the garment is an outward expression of an inward commitment to follow the Savior."[3] The garment is not "magic underwear" that keeps us from any physical harm, but faithfully keeping our covenants does protect us from the spiritual power of the evil one.

Anointed and Clothed

In the Old Testament, two kinds of people "put on Christ"—kings and priests. The Greek word *Christos* (*Meshiach* or *Messiah* in Hebrew) means "Anointed One." In the Old Testament, both kings and priests were anointed. They represented the Lord to the people with an extra measure of His Spirit. We read of David that "Samuel took the horn of oil, and anointed him in the midst of his brethren: and the Spirit of the Lord came upon David from that day forward" (1 Samuel 16:13).

The restoration of the temple endowment and covenants in our day allows the Lord to do what He has always intended. He did not want just the sons of Aaron anointed and clothed to enter into His presence and to be His representatives to the world. He wanted a kingdom of priests and priestesses. In our day priesthood in the temple is not about offices that are only given to men. As we put on Christ in temple ordinances, we are all given His name and nature. Christ is the Holy One, the King of Israel, the Great High Priest. In the ordinance of the endowment, we are all clothed in the garment of the Holy Priesthood and we all wear the robes of the Holy Priesthood.

Moses Calls Aaron to the Ministry, *by Harry Anderson*

Having been anointed and endowed, we all can go forth to do His priesthood work of loving and blessing our Heavenly Father's children throughout the world. As President Russell M. Nelson taught the sisters of the Church, "From those covenants flows an endowment of His priesthood power upon you."[4] Christ is the Great High Priest, and in the temple, we accept His invitation to more fully take His name upon us. We leave the world to go to the temple so that we can then be sent out in His name as His "kingdom of priests [and priestesses]" (Exodus 19:6).

As Moses prepared the people for worshipping the Lord in the tabernacle, he received specific detailed instructions about the dress of the priests. To be in the presence of the Lord they needed to be holy even as the Lord was holy. That holiness was manifest in what they wore.

Moses was told, "For Aaron's sons thou shalt make coats, and thou shalt make for them girdles, and bonnets shalt thou make for them, for glory and for beauty. . . . And thou shalt make them linen breeches to cover their nakedness; from the loins even unto the thighs they shall reach" (Exodus

28:40–42). They were to be clothed, anointed, consecrated, and sanctified. They were to represent the Lord, the Anointed One.

Connected with their washing and clothing was an ordinance of anointing: "Then shalt thou take the anointing oil, and pour it upon his head, and anoint him. And thou shalt bring his sons, and put coats upon them. And thou shalt gird them with girdles, Aaron and his sons, and put the bonnets on them" (Exodus 29:7–9). As part of the endowment we are ritually washed, anointed, and clothed with the temple garment, and we also wear special ceremonial clothing.

Worship

The priests' anointing and clothing prepared them for their priesthood service. The Lord stresses the garments' role in their ministry: "And thou shalt put upon Aaron the holy garments, and anoint him, and sanctify him; *that he may minister unto me in the priest's office*. And thou shalt bring his sons, and clothe them with coats: And thou shalt anoint them, as thou didst anoint their father, *that they may minister unto me in the priest's office*" (Exodus 40:13–15; emphasis added).

Under the law of Moses, the priests foreshadowed Christ, the Anointed One, in offering up sacrifices to atone for the sins of the people. The priests represented the Lord and helped to keep the temple and the people holy so that the Lord's presence could be there. Daily worship was required to reconcile individuals who came bringing sacrifices.

With the Melchizedek Priesthood and the new and everlasting covenant restored in our day, we no longer offer up animals but rather "a broken heart and a contrite spirit" (3 Nephi 9:20). Today it is not just the descendants of Aaron who are anointed and make sacrifices, but all endowed Church members.

As His anointed servants, how do we dress to participate in this worship? Aaron and his sons had holy garments put upon them "that they [might] minister unto [the Lord] in the priest's office" (Exodus 40:15). As we participate in the ordinances of the temple, we also put on the robes of the Holy Priesthood. And as we serve the Lord in our daily lives, we ritually put on Christ as we wear the temple garment.

Offering Ourselves

Just as Christ offered Himself as a sacrifice on our behalf, we are to offer ourselves. Paul explained: "I beseech you therefore, brethren, by the mercies of God, that ye present your bodies a living sacrifice, holy, acceptable unto God, which is your reasonable service [another word for 'worship']" (Romans 12:1). Paul then explained the transformation we experience as we present our bodies as a living sacrifice: "And be not conformed to this world: but be ye transformed by the renewing of your mind, that ye may prove what is that good, and acceptable, and perfect, will of God" (Romans 12:2).

God wants to give us all that He has and all that He is, but we have to give up other ways of being to take on His name and nature. Becoming like Christ intrinsically involves sacrifice, giving something up and making something holy. Changing our clothing because we have been endowed is a very practical and tangible kind of sacrifice.

Sacrifice is transformational if done with a broken heart and a contrite spirit. In giving away our sins, we can come to know Christ (see Alma 22:18). Every day there are ways in which we can choose to conform our lives to God's will. As we sacrifice whatever we want for what He wants, we come to be like Him.

Paul helps us see the connection between putting on Christ and how we use our bodies: "But put ye on the Lord Jesus Christ, and make not provision for the flesh, to fulfil the lusts thereof" (Romans 13:14). "Lusts" here can clearly refer to sexual temptation. A roommate once insightfully remarked that hopefully a person would stop and think before taking off the garment to break the law of chastity. Reminding us of our covenants is one way that the temple garment "provides protection against temptation and evil."[5]

But "lusts" can also refer to anything we seek after, anything we want that is different than what God wants. Putting on Christ is learning to put our own will on the altar, day after day. To receive His name and nature, we have to be willing to let go of what we want when it differs from what He asks. Amaleki framed this invitation powerfully: "And now, my beloved brethren, I would that ye should come unto Christ, who is the Holy One of Israel, and partake of his salvation, and the power of his redemption. Yea, come unto him, and offer your whole souls as an offering unto him, and continue in fasting and praying, and endure to the end; and as the Lord liveth ye will be saved" (Omni 1:26).

In the ordinances and covenants of the temple, Christ's salvation and the power of His redemption are offered to us, but we must choose to partake of them. We must choose to put them on. We can choose to worship daily in all that we do as we go about our lives clothed in the garment of the Holy Priesthood.

The Latter-day Opportunity

The lives of the ancient priests in Old Testament times can be hard to imagine. One evening serving in the temple, I read a passage that helped bring the priests' experience to life for me. I had served as an ordinance worker for close to ten years, and that evening I had a few minutes in the ordinance workers' study room during my break. I randomly opened the Bible and read in Ezekiel 44 a long list of requirements for the priests: "And it shall come to pass, that when they enter in at the gates of the inner court, they shall be clothed with linen garments; and no wool shall come upon them, whiles they minister in the gates of the inner court, and within. They shall have linen bonnets upon their heads, and shall have linen breeches upon their loins" (vv. 17–18).

The lives of the priests were constrained and circumscribed. They had to watch themselves all the time to maintain the holiness that would allow them to represent the Lord to His people and to do His work of reconciliation among them. The priests were the ones who had to demonstrate holiness with everything that they did. The tribe of Levi didn't even have an inheritance of land, unlike all the other tribes. Their lives revolved around serving God.

But what I read next helped everything make sense: "And it shall be unto them for an inheritance: I am their inheritance: and ye shall give them no possession in Israel: I am their possession" (v. 28). As the priests gave their lives to serve the Lord, they were able to receive all that He had. The Lord wants to give us Himself.

To me, the gift of wearing the garment of the Holy Priesthood is being covered with the love of Christ, "who gave himself for us, that he might redeem us from all iniquity, and purify unto himself a peculiar [or purchased] people, zealous of good works" (Titus 2:14). Christ gave Himself for us, but we have to choose to receive Him in the ordinances. We have to choose to receive Him in keeping our covenants. He wants to be our dearest possession. We can wear that love and that gift day and night for the rest of our lives.

CHAPTER 7

REDEMPTION: ENTERING THE PRESENCE OF THE LORD

"Savior, Redeemer of my soul,
Whose mighty hand hath made me whole,
Whose wondrous pow'r hath raised me up
And filled with sweet my bitter cup!
What tongue my gratitude can tell,
O gracious God of Israel."

—Orson F. Whitney, "Savior, Redeemer of My Soul"

I was in college when I first heard a comment about connections between the temples and Freemasonry. Many haven't heard about this, and for some the connection seems strange or uncomfortable. In recent years the Church has made important efforts to make lesser-known aspects of Church history more widely known. Part of this story is told in volume 1 of *Saints,* and there is also a Church History Topics essay on the subject.[1]

Long before the Joseph Smith Papers or *Saints* came out, I was in college working on a paper on Masonic influence in Mozart's opera *The Magic Flute* when I heard something about an early connection between the temple and Masonry. Later when I visited Nauvoo and saw the Cultural and Masonic Hall, I learned that Joseph Smith became a Mason shortly before he introduced the endowment in Nauvoo. In a time of great persecution, Joseph had hoped that belonging to a fraternal organization whose members were pledged to protect each other would offer him and the Saints additional safety. This was also the time when the temple endowment was introduced. To those skeptical of temple ritual, the timing of this development can look like a simple case of adoption.

To help us consider this connection between Masonry and the temple, here is some background from the Church History essay: "Freemasonry is a fraternal organization that grew out of centuries-old European trade guilds. Freemasons (or Masons) meet in lodges, where they ritually reenact a story based on the brief biblical account of a man named Hiram, whom Solomon commissioned to work on the temple in Jerusalem. During the reenactment, Masons advance by degrees, using handgrips, key words, and special clothing."[2] This historical context is helpful to understanding the time when the endowment ceremony was first presented.

Heber Kimball was one of the first people to participate in the endowment ceremony, and "some aspects of the ordinance reminded [him] of Masonic ceremonies. In Freemasonry meetings, men acted out an allegorical story about the architect of Solomon's temple. Masons learned gestures and words they pledged to keep secret, all of which symbolized that they were building a solid foundation and adding light and knowledge to it by degrees." But unlike the Masonic rituals, "the endowment was a priesthood ordinance meant for men and women, and it taught sacred truths not contained in Masonry, which Heber was eager for others to learn."[3]

Ambiguity and Clarity

For those who view the endowment as the creative vision of a nineteenth-century genius, the historical environment and Joseph's mind are all that are needed to explain it. For those who see Joseph Smith as the Lord's prophet through whom the Lord restored ordinances that are part of the covenant path leading back to God, there are very different questions to ask. We know that Joseph came to believe that Masonic rituals contained elements of an ancient endowment, just as other churches also had remnants of spiritual truth.[4] We do not have to believe in the antiquity of Masonic rituals, but it helps to know what Joseph believed and experienced to understand the historical context in which the temple endowment was introduced. Trusting that the Lord spoke through Joseph, many ask the question, "How much did Joseph's experience with the Masons shape what and how the Lord revealed for the temple ordinances?"

There are different approaches to the historical question of how much Masonry influenced the revealed temple ordinances. Did the Lord give His message by using some of a symbolic language that the early Saints could understand? Did learning the symbolic language of Freemasonry prepare Joseph to be taught the new symbolic language of the temple? We may not know the answer to these historical questions, but knowing that the Lord was the one communicating the message gives clarity about *whom* we are listening to at the temple.

We learn from Nephi that "the Lord God giveth light unto the understanding; for he speaketh unto men according to their language, unto their understanding" (2 Nephi 31:3). For me, having thought through these issues and seeing how the Lord speaks to us in our own language, I am less concerned about the possibility of a shared symbolic language or shared components of one. *What* the Lord is trying to communicate is more important than *how* He communicates it.

Different Narratives

We can see the contrast of the ritual meaning of the endowment and the ritual meaning of Masonic ceremonies in the Church History essay: "Masonic ceremonies promote self-improvement, brotherhood, charity, and fidelity to truth for the purpose of making better men, who in turn make a better society. During temple ordinances, men and women covenant with God to obey His laws for the purpose of gaining exaltation through the Atonement of Jesus Christ."

There are some parallels in how each path is taught, but the nature of these paths differs significantly. Again, the Church History essay says, "Masonic rituals deliver stage-by-stage instruction using dramatization and symbolic gestures and clothing, with content based on Masonic legends. The endowment employs similar teaching devices, but it draws primarily upon the revelations and inspired translations given to Joseph Smith for its content."

The Masonic rituals symbolically put participants into a story that gives meaning to their lives and helps them be better people. But this story of the Masons, embodied in their ritual, is a different story than the gospel of Jesus Christ. The gospel message that we ritually enact in the endowment is the Father's plan of redemption and exaltation. We symbolically experience His creating a world for us and then providing us with Christ's atoning sacrifice as we make and keep covenants. The story of the temple is the invitation to come unto Christ and be perfected in Him.

Elder David A. Bednar testified, "The most sacred covenants and priesthood ordinances are received only in a temple—the house of the Lord. Everything that is learned and all that is done in the temple emphasize the divinity of Jesus Christ and His role in Heavenly Father's great plan of happiness."[5] As we choose to look at the endowment with an eye of faith, the connections to Christ start to come into place. The liturgy, the temple's story told through ritual action, is the story of the plan of redemption.

As we worship in the temple, we remember what story we are really in. Enacting the ritual progression of redemption orients us and enables us to live out this deepening conversion and sanctification in our lives.

What Is the Story of Our Journey?

The story of the plan of redemption starts before the beginning of the world. In the temple we are taught the big picture of mortality. Through our participation in the temple liturgy, we ritually and symbolically participate with Adam and Eve in leaving God's presence and moving into a fallen world. Mortality after the Fall might be compared to getting amnesia. We know that we are here, but we don't know how we got here. We don't know our story.

Authorized Messengers

In both the endowment and in our lives, how do we learn which story we really are in? How do we learn the meaning of our actions? Revelation. The Lord sends authorized messengers to reveal the story we're in, to reveal the meaning of our lives and the journey we are on. Angels and apostles are sent to reveal what we *could not* know on our own. The Greek *angelos* means "messenger." In Greek, an *apostolos* is "one sent forth."

We need authorized messengers to reveal the story we are in and how to progress on our journey. Adam and Eve fell from the presence of God, and they didn't know the meaning of their lives. Without messengers they didn't know the meaning of their actions. God wants us to know why we're here. By receiving revelation through His messengers, we are connected to Him. "God conversed with men, and made known unto them the plan of redemption, which had been prepared from the foundation of the world" (Alma 12:30). As we are obedient to what we are given and keep seeking God, His plan of redemption becomes clearer.

LET'S TALK ABOUT TEMPLES AND RITUAL

Sacrifices

Until they received additional revelation from authorized messengers, Adam and Eve didn't know why they were sacrificing. The messengers taught them that their worship was part of the plan of redemption: "Then the angel spake, saying: This thing is a similitude of the sacrifice of the Only Begotten of the Father, which is full of grace and truth. Wherefore, thou shalt do all that thou doest in the name of the Son, and thou shalt repent and call upon God in the name of the Son forevermore" (Moses 5:7–8).

Then with this covenant, they were given a gift that more fully revealed Christ and His role in our salvation: "And in that day the Holy Ghost fell upon Adam, which beareth record of the Father and the Son, saying: I am the Only Begotten of the Father from the beginning, henceforth and forever, that as thou hast fallen thou mayest be redeemed, and all mankind, even as many as will" (Moses 5:9). Knowing the plan of redemption puts everything into perspective. It shows us the big picture, the story we are in.

The temple teaches of the Father's love in giving us a Savior who precedes this mortal life and continues through eternity. As Elder Jeffrey R. Holland taught, "In the premortal councils of heaven, God had promised Adam and Eve (and all the rest of us) that help would come from His pure, unblemished Firstborn Son, the Lamb of God 'slain from the foundation of the world,' as the Apostle John would later describe Him. By offering their own little symbolic lambs in mortality, Adam and his posterity were expressing their understanding of and their dependence upon the atoning sacrifice of Jesus the Anointed One. Later, the wilderness tabernacle would become the setting for this ordinance and, after that, the temple that Solomon would build."[6] The worship we give, the sacrifices we offer, are part of our process of redemption and connect us to

Christ's atoning sacrifice. He has power to redeem us all, if that is what we want and choose by making and keeping covenants.

Other Voices

While the authorized messengers of the Lord testify of the atoning sacrifice of Christ and show us how to worship, to live lives of repentance, to be obedient, and to sacrifice, other voices tell us not to believe the message we are being given. "And Satan came among them, saying: I am also a son of God; and he commanded them, saying: Believe it not; and they believed it not, and they loved Satan more than God. And men began from that time forth to be carnal, sensual, and devilish" (Moses 5:13). When we change our worship, we change our way of being.

Explaining why we need the Restoration, the Lord taught: "And the arm of the Lord shall be revealed; and the day cometh that they who will not hear the voice of the Lord, neither the voice of his servants, neither give heed to the words of the prophets and apostles, shall be cut off from among the people" (Doctrine and Covenants 1:14). Being His people is only possible as we hear and follow His servants.

If we leave the Lord's covenants and ordinances, we leave the path for our walk back home. "For they have strayed from mine ordinances, and have broken mine everlasting covenant; They seek not the Lord to establish his righteousness, but every man walketh in his own way, and after the image of his own god, whose image is in the likeness of the world, and whose substance is that of an idol, which waxeth old and shall perish in Babylon, even Babylon the great, which shall fall" (Doctrine and Covenants 1:15–16). Everyone worships something, and if we do not worship God in His way, then we cut ourselves off from the Way and the Life that He offers.

Redemption through the Blood of Christ

The temple's message of redemption has been expressed in different ways throughout time, but we need to learn to see it in the ordinances of our day. This message of how the covenants and ordinances bring us to a godly way of being through the application of Christ's atoning sacrifice is so important that Moroni ends the Book of Mormon with it:

> Yea, come unto Christ, and be perfected in him, and deny yourselves of all ungodliness; and if ye shall deny yourselves of all ungodliness, and love God with all your might, mind and strength, then is his grace sufficient for you, that by his grace ye may be perfect in Christ; and if by the grace of God ye are perfect in Christ, ye can in nowise deny the power of God.
>
> And again, if ye by the grace of God are perfect in Christ, and deny not his power, then are ye sanctified in Christ by the grace of God, through the shedding of the blood of Christ, which is in the covenant of the Father unto the remission of your sins, that ye become holy, without spot. (Moroni 10:32–33)

CHAPTER 8

THE GIFT: ENDOWMENT OF POWER

*"How silently, how silently
The wondrous gift is giv'n!
So God imparts to human hearts
The blessings of his heav'n."*
—Phillips Brooks, "O Little Town
  of Bethlehem"

Moroni stressed that in coming unto Christ, we need to *lay hold* upon every good gift: "And again I would exhort you that ye would come unto Christ, and lay hold upon every good gift, and touch not the evil gift, nor the unclean thing" (Moroni 10:30). Salvation is free; it is a gift, but we have to choose to receive it and to reject anything that will take us down another path.

In the temple endowment we ritually accept the invitation to receive the redemption and exaltation offered in Christ. President Russell M. Nelson gave a witness of this invitation: "These truths I know: God, our Heavenly Father, wants *you* to choose to come home to Him. His plan of eternal progression is not complicated, and it honors your agency. You are free to choose who you will be—and with whom you will be—in the world to come!"[1] We can't choose for other people, but we can choose for ourselves to accept the invitation to return home to our Heavenly Parents.

Though it is our choice to receive, we do not choose how the Lord gives His gift. In this chapter I will explore the question of why there have been changes to the endowment ceremony over time and also address the gift of priesthood power to both women and men in the endowment. For both topics, it helps to think through the gift that the Lord gives us in the endowment and how He chooses to give it.

A Gift

President Brigham Young spoke of the gifts of knowledge and power that we are given in the presentation of the endowment: "Let me give you a definition in brief. Your endowment is, to receive all those ordinances in the House of the Lord, which are necessary for you, after you have departed this life, to enable you to walk back to the presence of the Father, passing the angels who stand as sentinels, being able to give them the key words, the signs and tokens, pertaining to the holy Priesthood, and gain your eternal exaltation in spite of earth and hell."[2] As we come unto Christ, we are able to receive the enabling power that He wants to give us. This power comes with knowledge of Him, knowledge that will enable us to return back to the presence of God.

Additional insight into the endowment comes when we think of an endowed chair or setting up an "endowment" for an organization, which involves an enormous financial sum. The amount of the gift, of the endowment, is so large that people never need touch the principal but can fund everything they need with the interest alone. An endowment never runs out.

Same Message, Changes in Communication

We know from revelation that the blessings and covenants we receive in the temple endowment were available in ancient days. But the scriptures also describe differences in the ordinances over time. The Lord clothed Adam and Eve with coats of skins (see Genesis 3:21; Moses 4:27). After Adam and Eve left the garden, the Lord "gave unto them commandments, that they should worship the Lord their God, and should offer the firstlings of their flocks, for an offering unto the Lord" (Moses 5:5).

Abraham also sacrificed, and we learn that he was also given an external mark to signify his covenant relationship with the Lord: "This is my covenant, which ye shall keep, between me and you and thy seed after thee; every man child among you shall be circumcised. And ye shall circumcise the flesh of your foreskin; and it shall be a token of the covenant betwixt me and you" (Genesis 17:10–11). In Hebrew, the verb translated as "to make" a covenant literally means "to cut" a covenant.

The Lord later established the Aaronic, or Levitical, covenant with Israel at Sinai. In this era, circumcision continued to be the external sign of the covenant. Animal sacrifice was continued but with far more nuance than in earlier days—the priests needed a handbook to keep track of it all, resulting in the book of Leviticus. After Christ's mortal ministry, baptism replaced circumcision as the sign of the covenant and animal sacrifice was done away.

Revealed commands to worship and make covenants have always pointed to Christ, but how these covenants have been expressed has changed at different times. Sacrifice has always been part of the message. Being set apart as His people and being given a name have also always been part of the process. God speaks to us in our situation and context. He wants to communicate the message of salvation, but there have been adjustments in how that message is communicated through the ordinances.

The Restoration Is a Process

For some, the fact that temple ordinances have been changed over time can be confusing and frustrating. It helps to remember that the Restoration is a process; it is continuing. The Lord is communicating to His servants, but as always, He uses their language and reveals what they are able to receive at any given place and time. While we look back to the early days of the Restoration with gratitude for all that was revealed, it is refreshing to remember that the Lord continues to reveal His truths to us, and He modifies the temple ordinances to speak to us in our day.

President Russell M. Nelson reminded us: "After administering the endowment to Brigham Young in May 1842, Joseph told Brigham, 'This is not arranged right, but we have done the best we could under the circumstances in which we are placed, and I wish you to take this matter in hand and organize and systematize all these ceremonies.'"[3] My sense of the continuing Restoration has helped me feel grateful to see elements of the presentation of the endowment change over time.

Serving as an ordinance worker also helped me learn how to respond to changes. I got better at adapting to change since I had to put it into regular practice. The other ordinance workers and I had weekly training meetings before our shifts at the temple started where we learned the proper way of doing things. When I started, there were certain times when we were supposed to stand during the presentation of the endowment, but then that was modified, and then later modified again. We had to pay close attention each week and not go on autopilot, assuming we knew how things were done. Some changes in protocol were Churchwide, while some came under the direction of different temple presidents (I served under four temple presidents). The principle of careful obedience was always the same, but the directions and procedures changed frequently and sometimes rapidly.

Just as we change as we progress, the development of the presentation of the temple ordinances has also been a gradual and ongoing process. President Nelson taught, "From [the time of Brigham Young] forward, temple ordinances were gradually refined. President Harold B. Lee explained why procedures, policies, and even the administration of temple ordinances continue to change within the Savior's restored Church. President Lee said: 'The principles of the gospel of Jesus Christ are divine. Nobody changes the principles and [doctrine] of the Church except the Lord by revelation. But methods change as the inspired direction comes to those who preside at a given time.'[4] The message of the gospel of Jesus Christ is constant, but how that is communicated can change over time.

The Lord communicates with us through the symbolic language of the temple. As culture changes, the meaning of language changes, both verbally and symbolically. Some ways of expressing things that might have made sense in the nineteenth or the twentieth century but would now be distracting or disconcerting have been removed. Components that are not central to the gospel message and may have been part of earlier cultural or historical understandings can drop off. The Lord wants His message of redeeming love to be clear and unmistakable.

The Lord wants to speak clearly to us today and may adjust how He communicates in the future. As President Nelson explained, "Current adjustments in temple procedures, and others that will follow, are continuing evidence that the Lord is actively directing His Church. He is providing opportunities for each of us to bolster our spiritual foundations more effectively by centering our lives on Him and on the ordinances and covenants of His temple. When you bring your temple recommend, a contrite heart, and a seeking mind to the Lord's house of learning, *He* will teach you."[5]

Priesthood Power

As we are willing to give ourselves to God in making and keeping covenants, we are given an endowment of priesthood power, "the power of godliness" (Doctrine and Covenants 84:20). As part of the ongoing Restoration, President Nelson has emphasized how, through the temple, Melchizedek priesthood blessings and power are given to both women and men: "Because the Melchizedek Priesthood has been restored, both covenant-keeping women and men have access to '*all* the spiritual blessings of the church' or, we might say, to all the spiritual treasures the Lord has for His children."

He stressed that "every woman and every man who makes covenants with God and keeps those covenants, and who participates worthily in priesthood ordinances, has direct access to the power of God. Those who are endowed in the house of the Lord receive a gift of God's priesthood power by virtue of their covenant, along with a gift of knowledge to know how to draw upon that power."[6]

Nephi spoke of this priesthood power coming forth in the latter days: "And it came to pass that I, Nephi, beheld the power of the Lamb of God, that it descended upon the saints of the church of the Lamb, and upon the covenant people of the Lord, who were scattered upon all the face of the earth; and they were armed with righteousness and with the power of God in great glory" (1 Nephi 14:14). The endowment of priesthood power arms us with the power of godliness.

We see this Melchizedek Priesthood power and glory in the description of those who will reside in the celestial kingdom. All who inherit this glory will be kings and queens, priests and priestesses.

> They are they into whose hands the Father has given all things—They are they who are priests [and priestesses] and kings [and queens], who have received of his fulness, and of his glory; And are priests [and priestesses] of the Most High, after the order of Melchizedek, which was after the order of Enoch, which was after the order of the Only Begotten Son. Wherefore, as it is written, they are gods,

even the sons [and daughters] of God—Wherefore, all things are theirs, whether life or death, or things present, or things to come, all are theirs and they are Christ's, and Christ is God's. (Doctrine and Covenants 76:55–59)

"Not As the World Giveth"

Though the endowment of priesthood power that prepares us for celestial glory is extended to all in the temples, it is not tied to ordination or offices in the priesthood. Some, seeking greater representation and parity between men and women—as well as more opportunities to participate in Church administration—hope for women to be ordained to priesthood offices. Earthly priesthood offices are tied to administration and are public by their very nature: Bishops sit on the stand, are publicly recognized, and have authority to administer to all in their ward; apostles govern the entire Church body and are ordained to be witnesses of the name of Christ in all the world.

We don't know why the organization of the Church is such that in mortality some have certain types of visibility and authority while others do not. But we do know that the power of godliness is quietly extended to all in the temples. This priesthood power is tied to salvation and exaltation rather than to temporary, mortal roles. The lack of priesthood ordination for women may be troubling or confusing for some, but the eternal priesthood gifts given in the temple offer us a chance to focus on the big picture, on what is required for salvation and exaltation; it is a chance to think about the difference between temporary roles and eternal gifts.

Christ taught that He gives differently than the world gives. "Peace I leave with you, my peace I give unto you: not as the world giveth, give I unto you. Let not your heart be troubled, neither let it be afraid" (John 14:27). The gift of the endowment is very much *not* as the world giveth. It is private not public. It is personal not paraded. It is internal not external.

For example, we wear the garment of the Holy Priesthood underneath our external clothing.

Christ asked the disciples which is greater: those who sit at the table or those who serve the ones at the table? After they confirmed what the world valued, Christ then taught that He came to serve and not to be served. "I am among you as he that serveth" (Luke 22:27). The revelation of the divine nature is a radical inversion of the world's values and priorities.

While ordination to priesthood office allows men to publicly perform ordinances outside of the temple and permits them to enter the temple, women's roles as ordinance workers and participants in the greater Melchizedek Priesthood ordinances of the temple (the initiatory, endowment, and sealing ordinances) are privately executed. President Nelson taught that with the restoration of the Melchizedek Priesthood and through the endowment, "in the holy temple [all] are authorized to perform and officiate in priesthood ordinances *every time* you attend."[7] He helped us see that the temple ordinances are Melchizedek Priesthood ordinances and that, having been endowed, we, both women and men, can "officiate" in temple priesthood ordinances through our worship. Officiating in these priesthood ordinances is part of the sacred and eternal gift we are given in the temple.

In choosing to receive what the Lord offers, we must trust in that private, sacred gift of the endowment. President Nelson explained, "The heavens are just as open to women who are endowed with God's power flowing from their priesthood covenants as they are to men who bear the priesthood. I pray that truth will register upon each of your hearts because I believe it will change your life. Sisters, you have the right to draw liberally upon the Savior's power to help your family and others you love."[8] God wants to give us His power, and as we worship in the temple, we feel that power in greater abundance.

THE GIFT: ENDOWMENT OF POWER

Perspective on Gifts and Change

For many of us, these changes in the understanding of priesthood power and authority have been striking. Speaking of the prophet, the Lord told the Church, "His word ye shall receive, as if from mine own mouth, in all patience and faith" (Doctrine and Covenants 21:5). This principle of how to receive the word of the Lord given through His prophets and apostles is a powerful one. It includes both faith that the Lord is speaking through them and patience with their personal limitations and historically contextualized frame of reference. It invites us to receive what the Lord offers through the mortals He has chosen to speak for Him.

Knowing there has been change over time to temple ordinances can cause several reactions. Without patience and faith one can become frustrated that there was not initially a clear and unalterable revelation. One can be suspect of changes that are different from what they were used to. One can be disappointed that additional revelation didn't offer all that had been hoped for.

For me, the invitation to receive the Lord's words through His servants in patience and faith is a hopeful and encouraging message. I know that we are imperfect, and the Lord is perfect. It is a relief to know that He can work through his imperfect servants, and it gives me hope that He can work through me. Most of all, it reinforces my commitment to accept what we are given now, to treasure the living communication from a Living Christ to His living servants. I know that as I seek to hear His voice through His servants and ordinances, I am empowered.

When we do not recognize or take time to hear the message of the Lord through the ordinances, it poses a danger to us. President Nelson warned: "Most certainly, the adversary does not want you to understand the covenant you made at baptism or the profound endowment of knowledge and power

LET'S TALK ABOUT TEMPLES AND RITUAL

you have received or will receive in the temple—the house of the Lord. And Satan certainly does not want you to understand that every time you worthily serve and worship in the temple, you leave armed with God's power and with His angels having 'charge over' you."[9]

But, in contrast, when we choose to *receive* the adjustments and new insights that come, we open our ears to the Lord. He wants to speak to us, if we have the faith and patience to listen. Speaking of changes to the administration of ordinances made during the COVID-19 pandemic, President Nelson taught principles that apply to all time: "Under the Lord's direction and in answer to our prayers, recent procedural adjustments have been made. *He* is the One who wants you to understand with great clarity exactly what you are making covenants to do. *He* is the One who wants you to experience fully *His* sacred ordinances. *He* wants you to comprehend your privileges, promises, and responsibilities. *He* wants you to have spiritual insights and awakenings you've never had before. This He desires for *all* temple patrons, no matter where they live."[10]

CHAPTER 9

GOD'S ORDER: THE NEW AND EVERLASTING COVENANT

"Fear not, I am with thee; oh, be not dismayed,
For I am thy God and will still give thee aid.
I'll strengthen thee, help thee, and cause thee
  to stand,
Upheld by my righteous, upheld by my righteous,
Upheld by my righteous, omnipotent hand."

—Attributed to Robert Keen, "How Firm a Foundation"

While some may think of the "new and everlasting covenant" narrowly in terms of marriage, the term actually refers to the fullness of the gospel of Jesus Christ—all of the principles and ordinances of the gospel. Elder D. Todd Christofferson taught, "The new and everlasting covenant is the gospel of Jesus Christ. In other words, the doctrines and commandments of the gospel constitute the substance of an everlasting covenant between God and man that is newly restored in each dispensation. If we were to state the new and everlasting covenant in one sentence it would be this: 'For God so loved the world, that he gave his only begotten Son, that whosoever believeth in him should not perish, but have everlasting life' (John 3:16)."[1] The new and everlasting covenant has been the Father's plan from before the world was created and is how we are tied to our Savior. It refers to how Christ helps us return to our Father to receive all that He has.

The new and everlasting covenant is called that because the gospel, with all its covenants and ordinances, is new for us in our dispensation, and in any dispensation in which it is restored. It is everlasting because it has been the path back to God from the beginning. The blessings of Abraham, Isaac, and Jacob are the blessings that God wants to give to all His faithful children. We make covenants and then continue to press forward in Christ on the covenant path.

Just as the presentation of the endowment is an "embodiment" or "unfolding" of the covenants made at baptism, the sealing ordinance in the temple is an *extension* of the covenant path that we have followed through the endowment. Seeing how all the ordinances connect us to Christ provides perspective and gives meaning to walking in His way.

The covenant path is a process of receiving the blessings that God wants to give us through Christ, and we can rest in the confidence that those who are faithful to what they have received will, in time, receive all of God's promised blessings. The Lord's promise is that "he that receiveth me receiveth my Father; and he that receiveth my Father receiveth my Father's kingdom; therefore all that my Father hath shall be given unto him" (Doctrine and Covenants 84:37–38).

Marriage and Godliness

As the extension of the covenant path, marriage has a critical role in our doctrine. Our distinctive understanding of Heavenly Parents gives us a unique view of marriage. In much of the early Christian tradition, celibacy was seen as an ideal practice because it was viewed as mirroring angelic or divine life. Through the Restoration we see God's nature differently; knowing we have Heavenly Parents who are embodied changes the meaning of families and sexuality within marriage.

THE NEW AND EVERLASTING COVENANT

Having families and living together in love prepare us to receive the blessings of eternal life because they are part of the nature of eternal life. Rather than believing that asceticism in a monastic order imitates the divine life, with the restored doctrine concerning Heavenly Parents, we understand that family life is part of the path to follow God. But we also know that not everyone experiences marriage and family in mortality. How can we think about temple marriage as part of the covenant path when many do not have the opportunity or desire to receive the blessings of this ordinance in mortality?

Focusing on Christ and His Promises

Focusing on Christ and His covenant promises can help when we or those we care about do not experience a covenant marriage or children in mortality or find it difficult to relate to the idea of exaltation in families. It is essential to remember that to be exalted, we must first be saved. To receive the fullness of the Father, we must first take upon us the name of Christ. These are truths that *all* can focus on, no matter how distant, or even foreign, the promise of exaltation may seem right now.

Instead of being distressed by how different the vision of exaltation is from we what are currently experiencing, we can focus on Christ. Both salvation and exaltation come through Christ. I believe that if we keep our focus on faithfulness to Christ and receiving the salvation that He offers through the ordinances we have received, we can, in time, come to believe and trust in the promise that exceeds understanding—we can receive all that the Father hath.

To keep perspective, we can focus on the foundation of the covenant path. The first principle of the gospel is faith in the Lord Jesus Christ. President Henry B. Eyring spoke about how faith and faithfulness will help us when we are uncertain of the future: "My promise to you is one that a member of the

Quorum of the Twelve Apostles once made to me. I had said to him that because of choices some in our extended family had made, I doubted that we could be together in the world to come. He said, as well as I can remember, 'You are worrying about the wrong problem. You just live worthy of the celestial kingdom, and the family arrangements will be more wonderful than you can imagine.'"[2]

An Order of the Priesthood

As Latter-day Saints we typically use the term *exaltation* in a very specific sense—to refer to the highest degree of the celestial kingdom, as explained in section 131 of the Doctrine and Covenants. There we learn that to obtain this degree of glory, one "must enter into this order of the priesthood" (v. 2). The idea of eternal marriage being a priesthood order is not an isolated concept in the gospel message. The priesthood order of temple marriage is a continuation of the process of entering into God's order through the ordinances.

Choosing to make covenants by participating in the ordinances of salvation is choosing to enter into God's order. Our sacred commitments to keep the laws of God in the new and everlasting covenant set us apart from the world. Sometimes we may not realize the significance of this. An analogy might be seen in a monastic order in which monks and nuns make lifelong vows that separate them from ordinary, lay people. By making temple covenants, we, like them, live lives that are bound by promises to not live as the world lives.

In Christ's order and through our covenant relationship with Him, He redeems us from being servants of sin so that we can experience the freedom and order of walking in the Lord's way. "But now being made free from sin, and become servants to God, ye have your fruit unto holiness, and the end everlasting life" (Romans 6:22). We are "ordered" by living our lives in obedience to God. This order is not oppressive but liberating because it connects us to the life that is in Christ. There is order in being connected to Christ and being able to bring forth good fruit.

In Christ's covenant order, we bring forth good fruit by living holy lives and making godly choices. We bring forth good fruit as we progress toward His kind of life, eternal life. Rather than being in a monastic order that is committed to celibacy, in the convent order of the temple, we commit to live the law of chastity, which applies to all, married and single. This law is a way of becoming holy as we seek to come unto Christ on the covenant path. Living a chaste life is something we can all promise to do, something we can all choose. Eternal marriage is the fruit God promises us, in His time, as we are faithful to what we have agency over. It is not something that we have to force ourselves into or panic about.

Christ's Order

We learn that the ordinances of the temple were given so that "they may grow up in thee, and receive a fulness of the Holy Ghost, and be organized according to thy laws, and be prepared to obtain every needful thing" (Doctrine and Covenants 109:15). When we choose to walk in His ways and follow His paths, we choose to be organized according to His laws. When we choose to stay connected to Christ through covenant faithfulness, we can grow up in Him and receive the fullness that He offers.

The idea of being organized according to God's laws is clearer when we understand that order is organic. There is an order to a tree, which is nourished by roots and leaves, allowing the branches to bring forth fruit. There is an order to the human body when it is healthy and thriving. All the parts are connected, and they support each other, allowing each other to succeed. We become part of the body of Christ when we are part of His covenant people. We are connected to Christ when we abide in the True Vine.

As we follow Christ and walk in His way, He puts us into His order and promises to be the author of our eternal salvation. Alma spoke to the people of the city of Gideon so they would have a "sense of your duty to God, that ye may walk blameless before him, that ye may *walk after the holy order of God*, after which ye have been received" (Alma 7:22; emphasis added).

Alma talked about those who, through their faithfulness in this order, were cleansed by Christ and returned back to God's presence: "Therefore *they were called after this holy order*, and were sanctified, and their garments were washed white through the blood of the Lamb. Now they, after being sanctified by the Holy Ghost, having their garments made white, being pure and spotless before God, could not look upon sin save it were with abhorrence; and there were many, exceedingly great many, who were made pure and entered into the rest of the Lord their God" (Alma 13:11–12; emphasis added). As we walk after the holy order of God, we can be transformed by the power of Christ's redemption, being made pure and entering into the rest of the Lord. Ultimately, through our faithfulness, His power will bring us not only to salvation but also to exaltation.

Challenges May Arise

I have a husband, but no children. Others have children, but no spouse. Some either can't imagine marrying or can't imagine being part of a heterosexual couple. Some are happily married, but to someone who doesn't share their faith and commitments. Some are in a marriage that feels far from celestial. Any of these circumstances could make the eternal promise of "exaltation in families" feel very distant. We may even be tempted to reshape the idea of exaltation into a form that is more closely connected to our current situation.

THE NEW AND EVERLASTING COVENANT

I know what it feels like to be married and to try to make that relationship more and more celestial, but I don't know from personal experience what the mortal version of an eternal family with children is like. For me it is faith in Christ and hope in His covenant promises that keep the promise real and relevant. Others are not currently living the covenant of temple marriage, having never married or having been divorced. For those who are divorced and worried about a previous temple sealing, it is important to recognize that we will not eternally be in a relationship that we do not wish to be in. Elder Gerrit W. Gong taught, "We know that covenants are binding and eternal only by mutual consent of the parties affected and when confirmed by a merciful heaven's manifestation of the Holy Ghost, which the scriptures describe as 'the Holy Spirit of promise' (Doctrine and Covenants 88:3)."[3]

But no matter our situation, the covenant that applies to all is what we choose to do with our bodies. We may not be accountable for others' choices, our feelings, or even our sense of identity, but a core moral principle is that we are agents, and we are accountable for our actions. One covenant we make is the law of chastity, which is articulated in the family proclamation: "The sacred powers of procreation are to be employed only between man and woman, lawfully wedded as husband and wife." I recognize that living this law for some entails enormous sacrifice and difficulty. The scriptural term *abiding*, discussed in the next section, brings us back to Christ and to trusting in Him, even when the path is difficult or the future seems unknowable.

Abiding in Our Covenants

There is a phrase in the Doctrine and Covenants that has a great deal to teach us about observing our covenants, no matter our mortal situation. We are told that "they who are not sanctified through the law which I have given unto you, even the law of Christ, must inherit another kingdom, even that of a terrestrial kingdom, or that of a telestial kingdom. For he who is *not able to abide* the law of a celestial kingdom cannot abide a celestial glory" (Doctrine and Covenants 88:21–22; emphasis added).

The key verb here is *abide*. One sense of *abide* is to "endure" or "sustain."[4] This is the sense used in Malachi 3:2, which looks ahead to the Second Coming and asks: "Who may abide the day of his coming? and who shall stand when he appeareth? for he is like a refiner's fire, and like fullers' soap." Section 88 of the Doctrine and Covenants seems to be using *abide* in this sense when it warns that "he who is not able to abide the law of a celestial kingdom cannot abide a celestial glory." Becoming holy prepares us to endure, or sustain, the holiness of the Lord's presence. This is the journey of the covenant path, making and keeping covenants to be able to enter into the presence of God.

A related meaning of *abide* is to "rest" or "dwell,"[5] which also points to being in the presence of God. I believe this sense of dwelling, remaining, continuing, being firm and immovable, is also very important to understanding this verse. Abiding in our covenant relationship is how we become holy and prepared to abide His presence. Remaining close to Christ and abiding in Him gives us nourishment, hope, and strength for the journey. As we are connected to the True Vine, we grow in holiness and confidence that our future with Him is worth whatever sacrifices we make here.

Sanctification through Christ

It seems significant to me that section 88 uses the word *abide* rather than *obey*. While obedience is required and emphasizes our agency, the concept of abiding suggests covenant faithfulness is maintaining a relationship rather than seeking to save ourselves. By keeping our covenants, we are allowing

THE NEW AND EVERLASTING COVENANT

Christ to save us. He will sanctify us as we abide in Him and His law.

I believe that the law of Christ, or "law of a celestial kingdom," that we need to "abide" is best understood as Christ Himself and His invitation to live in a covenant relationship with Him. It is the invitation He extends to "abide in me, and I in you. As the branch cannot bear fruit of itself, except it abide in the vine; no more can ye, except ye abide in me. I am the vine, ye are the branches: He that abideth in me, and I in him, the same bringeth forth much fruit: for without me ye can do nothing" (John 15:4–5). Christ wants to be connected to us, and we choose to keep that connection alive through our covenant faithfulness.

We choose where we wish to abide. We can continue to abide in our own carnal nature and fallen state or abide in Christ. In the living out of the new and everlasting covenant, abiding the celestial law and abiding in Christ, we continue the process of being sanctified by the reception of the Holy Ghost. Christ's love and sacrifice is tied to our potential to become like Him: "Who so loved the world that he gave his own life, that as many as would believe might become the sons [and daughters] of God" (Doctrine and Covenants 34:3). His power to make us fully into children of God, in His image, depends on our faith to abide in that covenant relationship. He is the Holy One, and as we abide His law and are sanctified by it, we become holy as well.

By abiding in covenant faithfulness, we are "abid[ing] the law of a celestial kingdom," and thereby we allow the law to sanctify us. We don't sanctify ourselves, but rather the sanctification comes from Christ, who is the Light and the Law. But we can't be sanctified if we do not choose to abide His law. He invites us to become holy, to become His sons and daughters, to take on His name and nature.

CHAPTER 10

THE PLAN: ALL INVITED HOME

"The dream of the poet, the crown of the ages,
The time which the prophets of Israel foretold,
That glorious day only dreamed by the sages
Is yours, O ye slumbering nations; behold!"
—Theodore E. Curtis, "Awake and Arise"

When I was in the missionary training center, one of my teachers had a wonderful way of bringing together what we then called the threefold mission of the Church. He drew a circle and said, "This is everyone." He then drew a line through the circle: one half is living; one half is dead. Then another line was drawn through one half: part of the living are Church members; most are not. The message? The Church exists to help everyone come unto Christ. It is wonderful to remember that no one is left out. But in 2018, I heard a one-sentence explanation of this principle that was electric and still echoes in my mind. President Russell M. Nelson explained: "Our message to the world is simple and sincere: we invite all of God's children on both sides of the veil to come unto their Savior, receive the blessings of the holy temple, have enduring joy, and qualify for eternal life."[1]

To some, the charge to offer temple ordinances to all who have ever lived seems hard to believe. In an age where we have a heightened understanding of how religion has been an instrument of colonialist oppression, some may hesitate to think that others should be like us. There is so much good in many traditions, so why would we think that everyone needs to be made a Christian? And then, on top of all those reservations, the scope of this project is staggering. I would suggest that we think of the vision of offering temple ordinances to everyone in terms of offering a map to all who have ever lived. No one needs to take the map, but for anyone seeking to get home, there is no other way.

Maps

Of course we know that a map is only a representation of reality, but yet we place a great deal of value on the correspondence between maps and reality. We value not running into dead ends of roads or mountain paths. We are grateful to have a guide that helps us find places to eat and get gas while driving in unknown territory.

Because, by their very nature, maps have selective representation, different maps capture different aspects of reality. Some maps are street maps, but others show data about climate, demographics, sound pollution, disease, gun violence, trees, birds, etc. (My husband and I are especially fond of maps of bird populations.) Different types of maps can be used together to help us enjoy and understand more of reality. Nevertheless, at times when we are presented with two competing versions of the same reality, we may want to know which is closest to the way things really are and which shows us the things of most importance. The focus and truth claims of maps matter if we really want to get to our destination.

Religious Maps

Many religious maps of reality point us to different dimensions of our human experience and can be complementary. We can appreciate nature with the Shinto map, we can be more attuned to the need to be free from jangling and discordant feelings with the Buddhism map, and we can appreciate the holiness of a day of rest and worship with the map of Orthodox Judaism. Each map can give us tools to live and navigate our lives because there is an internal logic between belief and practice. We act based on the information that the map of our belief system gives us.

If I didn't believe there was an afterlife, then my choices would be governed by what I sought to experience in mortality, whether it be a life of pleasure or one of noble humanitarian service. If, as in Islam and Judaism, I believed that forgiveness is possible purely because of the benevolence of a merciful God, then I would try to live devoutly in reference to that Being but wouldn't see the need to rely on a Redeemer and come unto Him. But, as a Christian, believing that I need a Savior to cleanse my sins and help me return to God, I need to answer the question of how I can receive that remission of sins.

Belief and Practice

Different answers have been given to that question. Different maps lead to different practices. In the second and early third centuries, there was great concern about postbaptismal sin. Tertullian said: "We are not baptized so that we may cease committing sin but because we have ceased, since we are already clean of heart . . . for he has feared to continue sinning, lest he should not deserve to receive [baptism]. . . . Grant, Lord Christ, that Thy servants may . . . know nothing of repentance nor have any need of it [after baptism]."[2] Is it any wonder that a practice of deathbed repentance and baptism developed from this belief? If you can only be cleansed once, then it's safest to wait until you're finished with sinning and with life.

Likewise, when baptism came to be doctrinally associated with removing the stain of original sin, then the practice of infant baptism made perfect sense. Belief and practice are connected. Beliefs and doctrine lay out a map for the believers to follow in life. The maps we choose to follow guide the path we go down.

The Map of the Temple

In the October 1995 general conference, President Gordon B. Hinckley said of temples, "These unique and wonderful buildings, and the ordinances administered therein, represent the ultimate in our worship. These ordinances become the most profound expressions of our theology."[3] So what is the theology behind temples, including the vicarious work for the dead, that includes "the most profound expressions of our theology"? What is the internal logic of ordinances and vicarious ordinances? What map does the temple lay out for the believer's path?

I suggest the answer can be found in one of the earliest statements of revelation in our dispensation. When the angel Moroni spoke to Joseph Smith, he told him that God had a work for him to do and then spoke of the coming forth of the Book of Mormon, wherein, "the fulness of the everlasting Gospel [is] contained" (Joseph Smith—History 1:34). President Russell M. Nelson taught, "The Book of Mormon provides the fullest and most authoritative understanding of the Atonement of Jesus Christ to be found anywhere. It teaches what it really means to be born again. From the Book of Mormon we learn about the gathering of scattered Israel. We know why we are here on earth. These and other truths are more powerfully and persuasively taught in the Book of Mormon than in any other book. The full power of the gospel of Jesus Christ is contained in the Book of Mormon. Period."[4]

The Fullness of the Gospel

We often use the term *gospel* in its expansive sense to describe all religious truth. In this broader sense we, with President Hinckley, can say to all, "Bring with you all that you have of good and truth which you have received from whatever source and come and let us see if we may add to it."⁵ Or, with President Brigham Young, "'Mormonism' includes all truth. There is no truth but what belongs to the Gospel." The gospel "incorporates every system of true doctrine on the earth, whether it be ecclesiastical, moral, philosophical, or civil."⁶ In this broader sense of religious truth, we certainly can live a fuller life by learning from many religions' maps. Layering these maps together deepens our sense of the richness of the human spiritual experience and the nature of holiness.

When we use the term *gospel* in this expansive sense, to include all spiritual truth, then the idea that the Book of Mormon contains the fullness of the everlasting gospel may not make sense. If the Book of Mormon contains the fullness of the gospel, why are there so many spiritual truths not mentioned in this book of scripture? Thinking about the "gospel" with this broad focus, we may set aside our focus on the Book of Mormon and instead prioritize the exciting new insights Joseph continued to receive throughout the early years of our dispensation and look for more spiritual truths that have yet to be revealed. But even then, when we add in additional truths, such as the degrees of glory, we might feel sad that we have many questions left unanswered or cheated to have such a sketchy map of things we want to better understand, like Mother in Heaven. If the "gospel" means all spiritual truth, then we might become frustrated that we don't have all the truth yet, and we certainly won't see it in the Book of Mormon.

A Narrow, Focused Map

But I believe that Moroni was speaking about a very narrow definition of *gospel* when he said that "the fulness of the everlasting Gospel" was contained in the Book of Mormon. He clarified his meaning when he said, "The fulness of the everlasting Gospel was contained in [the Book of Mormon], as delivered by the Savior to the ancient inhabitants." When we look at the teachings of the Savior in 3 Nephi, I believe we are given the fullness of the map back to the presence of God—how to return and partake of the fruit of the tree and how to have that grow up in us unto life everlasting (see Alma 32–33). The gospel as taught in the Book of Mormon is a very focused and simple map because pointing the way back home is its primary role.

In 3 Nephi 27, Christ speaks to the ancient inhabitants and clearly defines His gospel, giving them and us the map of how to return to the presence of God: "this is the gospel which I have given unto you—that I came into the world to do the will of my Father, because my Father sent me. And my Father sent me that I might be lifted up upon the cross" (vv. 13–14). The first aspect of the gospel is Christ's mission to offer His atoning sacrifice on our behalf. He then explained how we can return to the presence of God: "And no unclean thing can enter into his kingdom; therefore nothing entereth into his rest save it be those who have washed their garments in my blood, because of their faith, and the repentance of all their sins, and their faithfulness unto the end. Now this is the commandment: Repent, all ye ends of the earth, and come unto me and be baptized in my name, that ye may be sanctified by the reception of the Holy Ghost, that ye may stand spotless before me at the last day" (vv. 19–20).

Something essential happens when we wash our garments in His blood by receiving the gift of the Holy Ghost that can happen in no other way, and we must choose that cleansing through faith, repentance, and making and keeping covenants. The restored map of how to travel home shows how Christ's Atonement intersects with our choices to receive that gift.

The Key to the Map

Once we understand the core doctrine of the fullness of the gospel, that only in and through the atoning blood of Christ can we be cleansed, we have the interpretive lens to understand the gospel map and therefore the map of the ordinances of the temple. Knowing this doctrine is having the map of the path that returns us to the presence of God.

It is possible to know the map as an outside observer, recognizing the internal logic between beliefs about Christ's Atonement and agency and the practice that follows from them. The academic study of religious beliefs and practice and their internal logic is fascinating. My field is the history of Christianity, and I wrote my dissertation on the internal logic of the late-medieval concept of *compassio* and how that belief, that it was necessary to suffer with Christ to receive the merits of the Passion, shaped late-medieval devotional practices.

In addition to academically studying the map of religious belief, it is also possible to know the map as a believer. For me, this knowledge is my witness that the map of the gospel is true and that Christ's Atonement, when accepted by faith, repentance, and making and keeping covenants, will bring us back to the presence of God. This kind of knowledge is my testimony, a personal affirmation and witness that this map corresponds to reality. It is a powerful and comforting assurance.

But living the doctrine of Christ by exercising faith in Christ unto repentance and living to invite the Holy Ghost is more than *knowing* the internal logic of the map or even knowing of its correspondence to reality, it is *following* the path back to the presence of God.

This gospel map is laid out in the symbolism and function of the ordinances of baptism, the gift of the Holy Ghost, the sacrament, the endowment, and temple marriage. All these ordinances point to the power of Christ's Atonement. As we participate in these ordinances, we experience in practice the doctrine that it is only in and through the atoning blood of Christ that we can return clean and holy to the presence of God and receive all that the Father hath. As we choose to walk on the path mapped out by the fullness of the gospel, we take on the fullness of the name and nature of Christ.

All Invited Home

The map shows us the path to follow, but the map does not create the distance between us and our destination. We may believe that there is no distance to travel, that we are almost there and so we can do without the map. For example, some might wonder about the amazing people who have lived throughout time. Do they really need the ordinances performed for them vicariously? Didn't they live lives that are sufficient to prepare them to return home?

Living a mortal life of goodness and positively responding to the Light of Christ is a meaningful preparation for receiving the new and everlasting covenant. President Dallin H. Oaks spoke of such people: "Many who come in the eleventh hour have been refined and prepared by the Lord in ways other than formal employment in the vineyard. These workers are like the prepared dry mix to which it is only necessary to 'add water'—the perfecting ordinance of baptism and the gift of the Holy Ghost. With that addition—even in the eleventh hour—these workers are in the same state of development and qualified to receive the same reward as those who have labored long in the vineyard."[7] Their choices to live up to the light that they had created a disposition to take Christ's name upon them, but those choices are not a substitute for that covenant, for the "perfecting ordinance of baptism and the gift of the Holy Ghost." This does not mean that mortal lives lived without the gospel map have no meaning. The universal reach of the Light of Christ makes every human choice meaningful.

With each choice, all are moving either closer to or further from God. Section 84 of the Doctrine and Covenants describes this process and how when we draw close to God, He teaches us of His covenants: "The Spirit giveth light to every man that cometh into the world; and the Spirit enlighteneth every man through the world, that hearkeneth to the voice of the Spirit. And every one that hearkeneth to the voice of the Spirit cometh unto God, even the Father. And the Father teacheth him of the covenant which he has renewed and confirmed upon you, which is confirmed upon you for your sakes, and not for your sakes only, but for the sake of the whole world" (Doctrine and Covenants 84:46–48).

Even for the very best people who have walked on earth, the covenant is needed. The gospel map testifies that there is a gulf between us and our heavenly home that cannot be bridged without Christ. Without the gospel map we would not know how to become clean and holy to return to God's presence. Without the gospel map we might not even know that there was a presence to return to. The fullness of this gospel map is contained in the Book of Mormon, which teaches the doctrine of Christ more clearly than any other book of scripture.

President Nelson has taught us that "when you reach up for the Lord's power in your life with the same intensity that a drowning person has when grasping and gasping for air, power from Jesus Christ will be yours."[8] It is through a personal feeling of desperately needing help that we come to know Christ and come to trust the redeeming power that Christ offers. It is in those times that we know how desperately we need the gospel map.

The times in my life when I have cried as I prayed are sacred moments. In these times I have reached out for help with circumstances or, even more challenging, with my own weaknesses and sins. As I felt divine help, I came to know that the distance between me and God can be bridged and has been bridged by Christ. This is what Alma refers to as having "felt to sing the song of redeeming love" (Alma 5:26). The more alive this feeling is for us, the more excited we are to share the blessings of that redeeming love with those in the spirit world by doing vicarious work for them, the more we love repenting and treasure the gift of change, and the more grateful we are that all will be offered that gift.

President Joseph F. Smith was taught that the fullness of the gospel map is taught to all in the spirit world by "chosen messengers" (Doctrine and Covenants 138:31). The vision in section 138 of who will be offered the message of the gospel map indicates the plan is comprehensive. This message goes to "those who had died in their sins, without a knowledge of the truth, or in transgression, having rejected the prophets" (v. 32). All who have not yet received the good news of how to return to God through Jesus Christ will have an opportunity to receive it or to receive it again.

And what is this message shared in the spirit world? The simple and focused map of the doctrine of Christ found in the Book of Mormon. "These were taught faith in God, repentance from sin, vicarious baptism for the remission of sins, the gift of the Holy Ghost by the laying on of hands, and all other principles of the gospel that were necessary for them to know in order to qualify themselves that they might be judged according to men in the flesh, but live according to God in the spirit" (Doctrine and Covenants 138:33–34). God accepts all who are willing to exercise faith, repent, and covenant, whether or not the covenants are made vicariously.

The Path Home

The Father's plan has always been to invite all to come and partake of the fullness of celestial glory and exaltation. We are living in the time when that purpose is most fully being realized. The fullness of the gospel is God's map of how to make that journey. The vicarious ordinances of the temple are witnesses of the Father's plan of love. All who have ever lived are and will be offered an opportunity to know the map, to take hold of the Savior's outstretched hand, and to take the journey.

As Sister Bonnie Cordon taught, "Come unto Christ and don't come alone."[9] Just as Lehi partook of the fruit and naturally extended the invitation to his family, as we partake of the Savior's love through the ordinances of the temple, we want to share them with our family as well. Our hearts are turned to those on the other side of the veil who need these blessings that they can't receive without our help. We are grateful for the opportunity to find our ancestors and other deceased family through family history work. As Joseph Smith taught, neither they without us nor we without them can be made perfect (see Doctrine and Covenants 128:15). We take on God's nature of reaching out in love as we extend these blessings to others by doing vicarious temple work.

CHAPTER 11

THE WAY: KNOWING THE LORD

> *"Changed from glory into glory*
> *Til in heav'n we take our place*
> *Til we cast our crowns before thee*
> *Lost in wonder, love and praise."*
> —Charles Wesley, "Love Divine,
>   All Loves Excelling"

It's not uncommon to hear the complaint that it's not fair that people get to hear the gospel in the spirit world because then they will know for sure that there is life after death. There won't be any doubts for them, and so the choice will be easy. This concern comes from confusing testimony and conversion. President Dallin H. Oaks taught that it is "not even enough for us to be *convinced* of the gospel; we must act and think so that we are *converted* by it. In contrast to the institutions of the world, which teach us to *know* something, the gospel of Jesus Christ challenges us to *become* something."[1] Knowing information or knowing the truth of the gospel is necessary but not sufficient. Knowing that life continues after death is not the same as wanting to live the Savior's way and coming to know Him as we become like Him.

Receiving the message of the gospel by authorized messengers, in mortality or in the spirit world, is necessary but it is not enough. Even making these covenants is not sufficient.

President Ezra Taft Benson taught: "Besides the physical ordinance of baptism . . . , one must be spiritually born again to gain exaltation and eternal life."[2] The ordinances of salvation open the door for us, but we must choose to walk on the covenant path. Whether on this side of the veil or the other, each person has to decide if they want to walk in God's way, following the Savior and living His kind of life—obedient, submissive, self-sacrificing. Each person has to choose to receive the gifts that will help them become like Him: "as many as received him, to them gave he power to become the sons [and daughters] of God, even to them that believe on his name" (John 1:12).

Laying Hold upon Every Good Thing

The issue is not what we *know*, but who we *are*. The problem is what we want. In Moroni 7, Mormon explains that the Light of Christ makes it possible for everyone to know good from evil. The problem comes with what we want, what we choose. He tells us that "if ye will lay hold upon every good thing, and condemn it not, ye certainly will be a child of Christ" (v. 19). And that's where we all find ourselves stuck—knowing what we should do but not doing it. How do we change what we do? How do we change what we want? Mormon speaks directly to that: "how is it possible that ye can lay hold upon every good thing?" (v. 20). And then he points us to the good news—our hearts can be changed. And he tells us how.

Mormon explains that we need revelation. We need to know about Christ. "For behold, God knowing all things, being from everlasting to everlasting, behold, he sent angels to minister unto the children of men, to make manifest concerning the coming of Christ; and in Christ there should come every good thing. And God also declared unto prophets, by his own mouth, that Christ should come" (vv. 22–23). Angels, messengers, are sent to tell the good news, that "in Christ there should come every good thing." Eventually everyone who has ever lived will know that. That is the plan; that is why we share the gospel and why we share the ordinances.

But knowing is only the first step. We are agents, and we decide what we are willing to receive. Once we know, we each must choose to receive the life and power that is in Christ. Faith is a principle of action. Faith is a choice. How do we lay hold upon every good thing? How do we choose what is right? We choose Christ. We receive Christ.

Transformation

Christ came to save us from a way of being that is less than godly and to help us receive His way of being. Mormon taught: "And after that he came men also were saved by faith in his name; and by faith, they become the sons [and daughters] of God" (Moroni 7:26). Christ came to help us receive His name and His nature, and we are offered and can share that gift in the ordinances of the temple. By participating, we exercise faith on His name, allowing Him to more fully help us become as He is.

President Benson stressed that the ordinances are necessary but not sufficient and that we "must be spiritually born again to gain exaltation and eternal life," and he connected this principle to the Savior's teaching to Nicodemus. We usually focus on this passage in the Gospel of John to stress the need for baptism—what we *do*—but note the prophetic focus on what we need to *become*: "Our Lord told Nicodemus that 'except a man be born again, he cannot see the kingdom of God.'" (John 3:3). What we do will not be enough unless we are changed and become transformed through Christ.

President Benson then quoted from President David O. McKay's and President Spencer W. Kimball's commentaries on this statement to Nicodemus: "Of these words President

Kimball said, 'This is the simple total answer to the weightiest of all questions. . . . To gain eternal life there must be a rebirth, a transformation.' . . . President McKay said that Christ called for 'an entire revolution' of Nicodemus's 'inner man.' 'His manner of thinking, feeling, and acting with reference to spiritual things would have to undergo a fundamental and permanent change.'"[3] Conversion means change, and the temple was always designed to help us be transformed.

Before Christ came, people were told of Him and they had to choose to act on the revelation they received: "By the ministering of angels, and by every word which proceeded forth out of the mouth of God, men began to exercise faith in Christ; and thus by faith, they did lay hold upon every good thing" (Moroni 7:25). By faith in Christ, we lay hold of the gifts that Christ offers to us.

Faith unto Repentance

Exercising faith in Christ gives us power to lay hold upon every good thing. Faith in Christ is trusting that obedience leads to happiness. Faith in Christ is trusting that His way of living is the path to peace and joy in this life and eternal life in the world to come.

Faith unto repentance is key to conversion. If we're not repenting, we don't fully have faith. If we're not obeying, we don't fully have faith. When we believe on Christ's name, we choose to repent of all our sins.

Choosing to worship increases faith in Christ. Choosing to serve in the temple and to share the blessings of Christ's Atonement takes faith and increases faith. Choosing to keep our covenants both takes and increases faith. All these choices from faith produce change; they produce conversion.

Samuel the Lamanite taught, "If ye believe on his name, ye will repent of all your sins, that thereby ye may have a remission of them through his merits" (Helaman 14:13). When we really trust in His power, in His atoning sacrifice, in His commandments, and in His way of being, then we want to be redeemed more than anything else.

Amulek taught, "Thus he shall bring salvation to all those who shall believe on his name; this being the intent of this last sacrifice, to bring about the bowels of mercy, which overpowereth justice, and bringeth about means unto men that they may have faith unto repentance" (Alma 34:15). Christ's atoning sacrifice provides us the means to have faith unto repentance.

The ordinances of salvation are available to us *after we repent*, but they are also part of *how we repent*. Participating in temple ordinances helps us more fully change what we want and what we do. By exercising our faith to lay hold upon Christ in the ordinances, we are laying hold upon power to change. When we lay hold upon Christ in the ordinances, we are laying hold upon power to become increasingly like Him. President Russell M. Nelson taught, "Positive spiritual momentum increases as we worship in the temple and grow in our understanding of the magnificent breadth and depth of the blessings we receive there."[4]

Sources of Faith

Having made covenants, having become children of the covenant, our faith in Christ's redeeming power grows. Through our temple worship, as we experience the power of His redemption in the narrative of the ordinances, we are reminded of Christ's role as our Redeemer. Our confidence grows that He is our Kinsman-Redeemer and that He will come to rescue us when we make mistakes. We know He will help us be our best selves, redeeming us from our sins.

Our faith in Christ grows each time we participate in the ordinances of salvation, for ourselves and for the dead. Each of the ordinances allows us to more fully behold the Lamb of God, who takes away the sins of the world. Choosing to immerse ourselves in the gospel narrative, in the plan of salvation, changes our hearts and our minds. The map of the temple reorients us to what is real. The temple allows us to reset our hearts upon God.

As we feel the Father's love in the gift of His Son and Christ's love in offering Himself on our behalf, we want to receive that gift and come closer to Christ. "He doeth not anything save it be for the benefit of the world; for he loveth the world, even that he layeth down his own life that he may draw all men unto him" (2 Nephi 26:24). Christ's atoning sacrifice was given precisely so that He could draw us all unto Him, if we choose to respond with love and gratitude.

We are drawn to Him as we behold His gift in the ordinances of the temple and as we choose to receive it. Christ invites all to come and partake of the gift He freely gives. He wants all to "partake of his goodness" (2 Nephi 26:28, 33). He invites us to become more like Him as we share that gift with others through vicarious ordinances.

The Temple and Becoming Like Christ

One of the clearest teachings of how the temple allows us to "partake of Christ's goodness" came from President Howard W. Hunter. His invitation to "look to the temple of the Lord as the great symbol of your membership" resonated broadly. What we might not have caught was his vision of how central the temple is in accepting his invitation "to live with ever more attention to the life and example of the Lord Jesus Christ, especially the love and hope and compassion He displayed." President Hunter continued, "I pray that we will treat each other with more kindness, more patience, more courtesy and forgiveness."[5] When we see how these invitations are interconnected, we better appreciate the power of transformation offered in the ordinances and covenants of the temple.

Becoming godly, having our hearts changed by the love of God, is the reason we have been given the endowment. When I taught New Testament classes and we studied 2 Peter, I would play a clip of President Hunter speaking in general conference so the students could hear his explanation, in his own voice, of this connection between the temple and the invitation to take on the divine nature: "Let us study the Master's every teaching and devote ourselves more fully to his example. He has given us 'all things that pertain unto life and godliness.' He has 'called us to glory and virtue' and has 'given unto us exceeding great and precious promises: that by these [we] might be partakers of the divine nature' (2 Peter 1:3–4)." It is in the ordinances of the temple that we are given these "exceeding great and precious promises."

President Hunter gave us his witness of the power to be transformed that is offered in temples: "I believe in those 'exceeding great and precious promises,' and I invite all within the sound of my voice to claim them. We should strive to 'be partakers of the divine nature.' Only then may we truly hope for 'peace in this world, and eternal life in the world to come' (D&C 59:23)."

It was then that he said: "In that spirit I invite the Latter-day Saints to look to the temple of the Lord as the great symbol of your membership. It is the deepest desire of my heart to have every member of the Church worthy to enter the temple. It would please the Lord if every adult member would be worthy of—and carry—a current temple recommend. The things that we must do and not do to be worthy of a temple recommend are the very things that ensure we will be happy as individuals and as families."[6] Keeping our covenants allows us to receive the blessings of the endowment, to be transformed and be partakers of the divine nature.

LET'S TALK ABOUT TEMPLES AND RITUAL

As Frequently as Personal Circumstances Allow

For many Saints throughout the world in 1994, a one-time visit to the temple to make covenants was the most they could hope for, given the far distance they lived from temples. But President Hunter could see that regular temple attendance mattered because of the process of transformation that comes through that service. He encouraged: "Let us be a temple-attending people. Attend the temple as frequently as personal circumstances allow."[7]

In 1994, there were forty-six temples. In early 2021 in the middle of the COVID-19 pandemic, when many temples were still closed, President Nelson taught: "Keep your temple covenants and blessings foremost in your minds and hearts. Stay true to the covenants you have made."[8] In the very next breath, he said: "We are building now for the future! Forty-one temples are presently under construction or renovation. Just last year, despite the pandemic, ground was broken for 21 new temples!"

The vision that President Hunter had is now being fulfilled and will continue to be fulfilled. Before announcing another twenty new temples, President Nelson explained, "We want to bring the house of the Lord even closer to our members, that they may have the sacred privilege of attending the temple as often as their circumstances allow."[9] Frequent temple attendance has a powerful influence on us and our deepening conversion and transformation. After announcing those historic twenty temples, President Nelson explained: "Ordinances of the temple fill our lives with power and strength available in no other way. We thank God for those blessings."

Coming to Know Christ

Christ's Church has been restored in our day to help us each receive the gifts of transformation available through Christ. Because of the establishment of temples, we can participate in the priesthood ordinances we need and share them with those on the other side of the veil. All of us need these blessings to more fully come unto Christ and to become more like Him. Elder David A. Bednar explained, "Covenants and priesthood ordinances are central in the ongoing process of spiritual rebirth and transformation; they are the means whereby the Lord works with each of us from the inside out. Covenants that are honored steadfastly, remembered always, and written 'with the Spirit of the living God . . . in fleshy tables of the heart' provide purpose and the assurance of blessings in mortality and for eternity. Ordinances that are received worthily and remembered continually open the heavenly channels through which the power of godliness can flow into our lives."[10] As we serve the Lord, we come to resemble Him and to know Him more fully. His power of godliness can fill our lives, moving us to do and be better than we ever could on our own.

Paul explained that the Church exists "for the perfecting of the saints, for the work of the ministry, for the edifying of the body of Christ: Till we all come in the unity of the faith, and of the knowledge of the Son of God, unto a perfect man, unto the measure of the stature of the fulness of Christ" (Ephesians 4:12–13). Coming to the knowledge of the Son of God here means coming to be like Him, to take on the "measure of the stature of the fulness of Christ."

How can we know that we are on this path of conversion and transformation, that we are coming to know the Lord? Mormon said, "I judge that ye have faith in Christ because of your meekness" (Moroni 7:39). Christ invites us: "Take my yoke upon you, and learn of me; for I am meek and lowly in heart: and ye shall find rest unto your souls" (Matthew 11:29). In our temple worship we more fully learn of Christ, taking His name and nature upon us. Then, after we covenant, we continue to exercise our faith in Christ to worship and to serve as He asks; we continue to learn of Him. When we are meek, we are true disciples, apprentices who are willing to follow direction and change to become more like our Master.

Covenant Knowledge

The Lord revealed to Jeremiah that in the new covenant, knowledge of Him would fill the earth as it is embodied in His people: "But this shall be the covenant that I will make with the house of Israel; After those days, saith the Lord, I will put my law in their inward parts, and write it in their hearts; and will be their God, and they shall be my people. And they shall teach no more every man his neighbour, and every man his brother, saying, Know the Lord: for they shall all know me, from the least of them unto the greatest of them, saith the Lord" (Jeremiah 31:33–34). The Lord had a plan for this covenant knowledge to spread throughout the world, and it is being accomplished before our eyes as temples are built throughout the earth. More and more Saints can now have the law written in their hearts and bodies and come to know the Lord more fully through the experience of the temple.

Through our faithful service we take on His meekness and His godliness. During my years living in Laie, Hawaii, I had the privilege to serve with sisters and brothers who were transformed by their temple service. They sought to be in the temple many times a week, or at least once every week if they still had full-time employment. Those who made temple attendance and temple service a priority reoriented their lives to the Lord and blessed those who had not yet made those covenants. At the age of twelve, the grandson of an older Tongan sister who attended the temple every day told his father that rather than starting with a youth football team, he wanted to go do baptisms for the dead every day after school. He wanted the Savior's yoke more than a football uniform.

Elder Bednar has taught, "We take the Savior's yoke upon us as we learn about, worthily receive, and honor sacred covenants and ordinances. We are bound securely to and with the Savior as we faithfully remember and do our best to live in accordance with the obligations we have accepted. And that bond with Him is the source of spiritual strength in every season of our lives."[11] The temple allows us to be bound to Christ and have His power in our lives.

His Yoke

We don't need to understand everything to take Christ's yoke upon us. We don't have to have resolved every question or concern that we've ever had. We just need to trust Christ enough to accept His invitation to come unto Him, to learn of Him. He will help us along the path. If we are meek and humble enough to want to change and grow, He is there to help us. The gift of the Holy Ghost and the endowment of power come from Him to help us keep moving forward. These gifts provide us with the personal tutoring and direction we need for each step of the way. We just have to keep listening and following. He will lead us along.

Ascending

For nineteen years I was fortunate to live within a ten-minute walk of the Laie Hawaii Temple. In the architecture of this temple, like a few of the older temples, the message of ascension is very clear. This unusual architecture points to the message that is implied in the ordinance of the endowment. An endowment session starts in the creation room and then, during the progression of the ceremony, the company moves around an ascending spiral, higher and higher, from room to room. By the time we arrive at the celestial room, we have been through four different rooms. This message of progression, of coming unto Christ and being perfected in Him, is part of the endowment ceremony anywhere in the world, but being able to physically progress through that journey helped to emphasize the changes and the progress that was happening.

Perhaps this might tell us something about our lives. We might not always realize the progress that we're making as we are coming unto Christ. We do have to keep exercising faith and keep repenting day by day, but through the process of sanctification, we gradually repent of different things. We may feel like we're going around and around, but we're also ascending. As we continue to exercise faith in Christ, repent, take the sacrament, and listen to and follow the Spirit, we travel around and around, climbing upward, being drawn more and more fully to Christ. The temple maps out that journey for us, but we have to walk it as we live out the lives that we have covenanted to live.

From Glory into Glory

When I returned from my mission, a friend and I met each Friday afternoon to attend an endowment session every week. Walking together up Ninth East Street to the Provo Utah Temple every Friday oriented our lives. Setting that pattern of weekly temple worship was transformative. I still remember the feeling of growing in holiness as I went through an endowment session, being clothed "with the garments of salvation" and covered with the "robe of righteousness" (Isaiah 61:10). Brigham Young spoke of what we give up when we choose to receive the gifts the Lord offers us:

> I have heard a great many tell about what they have suffered for Christ's sake. I am happy to say I never had occasion to. I have enjoyed a great deal, but so far as suffering goes I have compared it a great many times, in my feelings and before congregations, to a man wearing an old, worn-out, tattered and dirty coat, and somebody comes along and gives him one that is new, whole and beautiful. This is the comparison I draw when I think of what I have suffered for the Gospel's sake—I have thrown away an old coat and have put on a new one.[12]

THE WAY: KNOWING THE LORD

We may not fully understand what we are becoming as we are reborn as Christ's spiritual children and joint-heirs, but worship in the temple helps us feel God's love, which draws us toward His way of being: holy, pure, and godly. "Behold, what manner of love the Father hath bestowed upon us, that we should be called the [children] of God: . . . it doth not yet appear what we shall be: but we know that, when he shall appear, we shall be like him; for we shall see him as he is. And every [one] that hath this hope in him purifieth himself, even as he is pure" (1 John 3:1–3).

ACKNOWLEDGMENTS

I am grateful to Lisa Roper, who both extended the invitation to write this book and continued to offer thoughtful feedback and suggestions through the writing process. I am also grateful for the anonymous readers whose feedback helped me greatly. I deeply appreciate family, friends, colleagues, and research assistants who took time to read and give important suggestions—Elizabeth Clark, Keith Lane, Lisa Spice, Lisa Rosenbaum Ishikuro, Terryl Givens, Hannah Faulconer, and Emma Belnap. Alison Palmer provided expert and thoughtful editing prior to production, and I am grateful for her. I particularly want to thank Michael P. Lyon's family who took time during the last days of his life to help me obtain his permission to use his beautiful illustrations.

In addition to all who helped with the book itself, I must acknowledge with gratitude faculty members with whom I studied ancient Near Eastern temples, particularly David Rolph Seely and Stephen D. Ricks. My heart is full of love and gratitude for all the fellow temple workers, matrons, assistant matrons, and temple presidencies with whom I served for many happy years in Laie, Hawaii. The goodness of the temple workers and patrons with whom I have associated has helped me feel Christ's love and presence in the temple.

FURTHER READING

The Role of Liturgy and Worship

Lane, Jennifer C. "Embodied Knowledge." *Element: A Journal of Mormon Philosophy and Theology* (March 2007): 61–71.

Smith, James K. A. *You Are What You Love: The Spiritual Power of Habit.* Grand Rapids, MI: Brazos Press, 2016.

Ancient Temples

Hamblin, William, and David R. Seely. *Solomon's Temple: Myth and History*, London: Thames & Hudson, 2007.

Morales, L. Michael, ed. *Cult and Cosmos: Tilting toward a Temple-Centered Theology.* Biblical Tools and Studies. Leuven, Belgium: Peeters, 2014.

Temple on Mount Zion Series. Salt Lake City: Interpreter/Eborn Books, 2014–Present.

Modern Temples

Bennett, Richard E. *Temples Rising: A Heritage of Sacrifice.* Salt Lake City, UT: Deseret Book, 2019.

The Temple and Freemasonry

Harper, Steven C. "Freemasonry and the Latter-day Saint Temple Endowment," in *A Reason for Faith: Navigating LDS Doctrine & Church History*, ed. Laura H. Hales. Provo, UT: Religious Studies Center, BYU; Salt Lake City: Deseret Book, 2016.

FURTHER READING

The Gospel and the Temple

Hafen, Bruce. "A Disciple's Journey." BYU devotional address, Provo, UT, February 5, 2008. https://speeches.byu.edu/talks/bruce-c-hafen/disciples-journey/.

Hafen, Bruce and Marie. *The Contrite Spirit: How the Temple Helps Us Apply Christ's Atonement*. Salt Lake City: Deseret Book, 2015.

Lane, Jennifer C. *Finding Christ in the Covenant Path: Ancient Insights for the Modern World*. Provo, UT: Religious Studies Center, Brigham Young University; Salt Lake City: Deseret Book, 2020.

From BYU's Religious Studies Center
Available at rsc.byu.edu

Belnap, Daniel L., ed. *By Our Rites of Worship: Latter-day Saint Views on Ritual in History, Scripture, and Practice*. 2013.

Colvin, Don V. *Nauvoo Temple: A Story of Faith*. 2002.

Hafen, Bruce C. "Peter, the Priesthood, the Temple, and Christ's Atonement." 2015.

Harper, Steven C. "Joseph Smith and the Kirtland Temple, 1836." 2010.

Holzapfel, Richard Neitzel. "The Nauvoo Temple, 1841." 2010.

Lane, Jennifer C. "The Lord Will Redeem His People: Adoptive Covenant and Redemption in the Old Testament." 2005 rev.; 1993.

———. "The Presence of the Lord." 2011.

———. "Redemption's Grand Design for Both the Living and the Dead." 2020 rev.; 2008.

———. "Sitting Enthroned: A Scriptural Perspective." 2018.

———. "The Whole Meaning of the Law: Christ's Vicarious Sacrifice." 2021 rev.; 2009.

———. "Worship: Bowing Down and Serving the Lord." 2013.

Madsen, Truman G., ed. *The Temple in Antiquity*. 1984.

Strathearn, Gaye. "'Holiness to the Lord' and Personal Temple Worship." 2009.

NOTES

Chapter 1, Leaving the World: Holiness to the Lord

1. Russell M. Nelson, "The Temple and Your Spiritual Foundation," *Liahona*, November 2021, 94; quoting Bible Dictionary, "Temple."
2. Ronald A. Rasband, "Recommended to the Lord," *Liahona*, November 2020, 23.
3. Sarah Jane Weaver, "Elder Bednar Speaks of the Washington D.C. Temple: 'It Is Not Just about This Building,'" *Church News*, April 18, 2022, https://www.thechurchnews.com/temples/2022-04-18/elder-bednar-speaks-of-the-washington-d-c-temple-it-is-not-just-about-this-building-251147.
4. Boyd K. Packer, *The Holy Temple* (Salt Lake City: Bookcraft, 1980), 144.
5. Jeffrey R. Holland, "The Message, the Meaning, and the Multitude," *Ensign*, November 2019, 7.

Chapter 2, Becoming His: Children of the Covenant

1. Russell M. Nelson, "The Temple and Your Spiritual Foundation," *Liahona*, November 2021, 94.
2. David A. Bednar, "Honorably Hold a Name and Standing," *Ensign*, May 2009, 98.
3. David A. Bednar, "Let This House Be Built unto My Name," *Liahona*, May 2020, 86.

Chapter 3, The House of the Lord: A Home for the Lord in Our Day

1. Russell M. Nelson, "The Temple and Your Spiritual Foundation," *Liahona*, November 2021, 94.
2. 2 Peter 1:4; Howard W. Hunter, "Exceeding Great and Precious Promises," *Ensign*, November 1994, 7–9.
3. *Saints: Volume 2, No Unhallowed Hand, 1846–1893* (Salt Lake City: The Church of Jesus Christ of Latter-day Saints, 2020), chap. 3; *History of the Church*, vol. 16, September 24 and 27, 1846, 49, 51; Brigham Young to the High Council at Council Point, September

NOTES

27, 1846, Brigham Young Office Files, Church History Library, Salt Lake City.
4. Nelson, "The Temple and Your Spiritual Foundation," 94.
5. Brad Wilcox, "His Grace Is Sufficient" (BYU devotional address, Provo, UT, July 12, 2011).

Chapter 4, Ritual Orientation: Sacred Time and Space

1. Jeffrey R. Holland, "The Message, the Meaning, and the Multitude," *Ensign*, November 2019, 7.
2. David A. Bednar, "But We Heeded Them Not," *Liahona*, May 2022, 15.
3. "Sacred Temple Clothing," Temples, The Church of Jesus Christ of Latter-day Saints, https://www.churchofjesuschrist.org/temples/sacred-temple-clothing?lang=eng.
4. "About the Temple Endowment," Temples, The Church of Jesus Christ of Latter-day Saints, https://www.churchofjesuschrist.org/temples/what-is-temple-endowment?lang=eng.
5. "About the Temple Endowment."
6. David A. Bednar, "Lehi's Dream: Holding Fast to the Rod," *Ensign*, October 2011, 34.
7. Neil L. Andersen, "Fruit," *Ensign*, November 2019, 117.
8. Ezra Taft Benson, "The Great Commandment—Love the Lord," *Ensign,* May 1988, 4.
9. Ezra Taft Benson, "What I Hope You Will Teach Your Children about the Temple," *Ensign*, August 1985, 8.
10. Dallin H. Oaks, "The Challenge to Become," *Ensign*, November 2000, 33.
11. Oaks, "The Challenge to Become," 34.
12. Oaks, "The Challenge to Become," 33.

Chapter 5, The Journey:
Continuing on the Covenant Path

1. Russell M. Nelson, "As We Go Forward Together," *Ensign*, April 2018, 7.
2. Elder D. Todd Christofferson explained the fulness of the Holy Ghost, saying, "The 'fulness of the Holy Ghost' includes what Jesus described as 'the promise which I give unto you of eternal life, even the glory of the celestial kingdom; which glory is that of the church of the Firstborn, even of God, the holiest of all, through Jesus Christ his Son' (D&C 88:4–5)." "The Power of Covenants," *Ensign*, May 2009, 23, note 5.
3. Harold B. Lee, *Teachings of the Presidents of the Church* (Salt Lake City: The Church of Jesus Christ of Latter-day Saints, 2000), 107.

NOTES

4. *General Handbook: Serving in The Church of Jesus Christ of Latter-day Saints*, 27.2, ChurchofJesusChrist.org.
5. "About the Temple Endowment," *Temples*, The Church of Jesus Christ of Latter-day Saints, https://www.churchofjesuschrist.org/temples/what-is-temple-endowment?lang=eng.
6. Harold B. Lee, *Teachings of the Presidents of the Church*, 107; emphasis added.
7. Jeffrey R. Holland, "Place No More for the Enemy of My Soul," *Ensign*, May 2010, 46.

Chapter 6, New Identity: Putting On Christ

1. "Garments," Gospel Topics, The Church of Jesus Christ of Latter-day Saints, https://www.churchofjesuschrist.org/study/manual/gospel-topics/garments?lang=eng.
2. David A. Bednar, "Let This House Be Built unto My Name," *Ensign*, May 2020, 85.
3. "Temples," Gospel Topics, The Church of Jesus Christ of Latter-day Saints," https://www.churchofjesuschrist.org/study/manual/gospel-topics/temples?lang=eng.
4. Russell M. Nelson, "Spiritual Treasures," *Ensign*, November 2019, 79.
5. "Temples."

Chapter 7, Redemption: Entering the Presence of the Lord

1. See *Saints: Volume 1, The Standard of Truth, 1815–1846*, (Salt Lake City: The Church of Jesus Christ of Latter-day Saints, 2018), 449.
2. "Masonry," Church History Topics, The Church of Jesus Christ of Latter-day Saints, https://www.churchofjesuschrist.org/study/history/topics/masonry?lang=eng.
3. *Saints: Volume 1,* 454–55.
4. Benjamin F. Johnson, *My Life's Review* (np: Johnson Family Organization, 1997), 85. There were differences within Masonic orders and change over time. Some forms had more Christian themes. See Michael W. Homer, *Joseph's Temples: The Dynamic Relationship between Freemasonry and Mormonism* (Salt Lake City: University of Utah Press, 2014), 47–51.
5. David A. Bednar, "Let This House Be Built unto My Name," *Liahona*, May 2020, 86.
6. Jeffrey R. Holland, "Behold the Lamb of God," *Ensign*, May 2019, 44.

Chapter 8, The Gift: Endowment of Power

1. Russell M. Nelson, "The Temple and Your Spiritual Foundation," *Liahona*, November 2021, 96.
2. *Discourses of Brigham Young*, comp. John A. Widtsoe (Salt Lake City: Deseret Book, 1971), 416.

NOTES

3. Nelson, "The Temple and Your Spiritual Foundation," 94.
4. Nelson, "The Temple and Your Spiritual Foundation," 94.
5. Nelson, "The Temple and Your Spiritual Foundation," 95.
6. Russell M. Nelson, "Spiritual Treasures," *Ensign*, November 2019, 77.
7. Nelson, "Spiritual Treasures," 78.
8. Nelson, "Spiritual Treasures," 77.
9. Nelson, "Spiritual Treasures," 78.
10. Nelson, "The Temple and Your Spiritual Foundation," 94–95.

Chapter 9, God's Order: The New and Everlasting Covenant

1. D. Todd Christofferson, "The Power of Covenants," *Ensign*, May 2009, 20.
2. Henry B. Eyring, "A Home Where the Spirit of the Lord Dwells," *Ensign*, May 2019, 25.
3. Gerrit W. Gong, "The Miracle of Covenant Belonging," *Ensign*, February 2019, 29.
4. Webster's 1828 Dictionary, "Abide," transitive.
5. Webster's 1828 Dictionary, "Abide," intransitive.

Chapter 10, The Plan: All Invited Home

1. Russell M. Nelson, "Let Us All Press On," *Ensign*, May 2018, 118–19.
2. Tertullian, *On Penitence*, 6–7, in *Treatises on Penance: On Penitence and On Purity*, trans. William P. Le Saint, *Ancient Christian Writers: The Works of the Fathers in Translation* (New York: Newman Press, 1959), 26–27.
3. Gordon B. Hinckley, "Of Missions, Temples, and Stewardship," *Ensign*, November 1995, 53.
4. Russell M. Nelson, "The Book of Mormon: What Would Your Life Be Like without It?" *Ensign*, November 2017, 62.
5. Gordon B. Hinckley, "The Marvelous Foundation of Our Faith," *Ensign*, November 2002, 81.
6. Brigham Young, *Teachings of Presidents of the Church* (Salt Lake City: The Church of Jesus Christ of Latter-day Saints, 1997), chap. 2.
7. Dallin H. Oaks, "The Challenge to Become," *Ensign*, November 2000, 34.
8. Russell M. Nelson, "Drawing the Power of Jesus Christ into Our Lives," *Ensign*, May 2017, 42.
9. Bonnie H. Cordon, "Come unto Christ and Don't Come Alone," *Liahona*, November 2021, 10.

Chapter 11, The Way: Knowing the Lord

1. Dallin H. Oaks, "The Challenge to Become," *Ensign*, November 2000, 32; see also David A. Bednar, "Converted unto the Lord, *Ensign*, November 2012, 106–9

NOTES

2. Ezra Taft Benson, "Born of God," *Ensign*, November 1985, 6.
3. Benson, "Born of God," 5.
4. Russell M. Nelson, "Now Is the Time," *Liahona*, May 2022, 126.
5. Howard W. Hunter, "Exceeding Great and Precious Promises," *Ensign*, November 1994, 8.
6. Hunter, "Exceeding Great and Precious Promises," 8.
7. Hunter, "Exceeding Great and Precious Promises," 8.
8. Russell M. Nelson, "COVID-19 and Temples," *Liahona*, May 2021, 127.
9. Nelson, "COVID-19 and Temples," 127.
10. David A. Bednar, "Let This House Be Built unto My Name," *Liahona*, May 2020, 86.
11. David A. Bednar, "With the Power of God in Great Glory," *Liahona*, November 2021, 29.
12. *Discourses of Brigham Young*, sel. by John A. Widtsoe (Salt Lake City: Deseret Book, 1941), 348.

INDEX

Aaronic Priesthood, 8–9, 20, 49, 75
Abide, 89–91
Abraham, 16, 17, 29, 43–45, 75
Aburto, Reyna I., 8
Adam and Eve, 69–70, 74–75
Afterlife, 86, 94–95, 101, 103
Andersen, Neil L., 41
Angels, 69
Animal sacrifice, 12, 75
Anointing, 5–6, 38, 59–61
Answers, finding, in temple, 1–2
Apostles, 69
Ascension, 113–14
Atonement: ordinances pointing to, 12–13; and returning to God's presence, 30–31, 97, 98–99; partaking of blessings of, 41; sacrifice and, 70–71; redemption through, 71–72; ordinances point to power of, 97–99; and faith unto repentance, 107
Authorized messengers, 69

Baptism, 50, 57–58, 94
Baptismal covenants, 8, 19, 50
Becoming, 33, 103
Bednar, David A., 19, 22, 34, 41, 58, 68, 111, 112–13
Belief, and practice, 94–95, 98
Benson, Ezra Taft, 43, 44, 104, 105

Book of Mormon, 95, 96–97
Bowing down, 40
Broken heart and contrite spirit, 61, 62–63

Celestial kingdom, 57, 78, 86, 90, 91
Change, 45, 53–54, 58, 104, 105–6, 109, 111. *See also* conversion; spiritual progress
Chastity, law of, 87, 89
Christofferson, D. Todd, 83
Church of Jesus Christ of Latter-day Saints, The, mission of, 92
Circumcision, 75
Clothing, 37, 38, 59–62. *See also* garment
Conversion, 45, 103, 106. *See also* change
Cordon, Bonnie, 102
Covenant knowledge, 112–13
Covenant path, 48–49, 84; willingness to follow, 52–53; continuing on, 53–54; faith as foundation of, 85–86; choosing to walk, 103–4
Covenants, 15–22; baptismal covenants, 8, 19; as orientation, 34; of endowment, 51; and entering God's order, 86; and divorce, 89; abiding in, 89–90; sanctification through keeping, 90–91; need for, 99–100; and

INDEX

spiritual rebirth, 111. *See also* new and everlasting covenant

David, 59
Death, peace regarding, 21–22. *See also* afterlife
Degrees of glory, 57, 78, 86, 90, 91
Discipleship, 35, 45–46, 111
Divorce, 89

Early Saints: commanded to build temples, 23–24; westward migration of, 27–28; faith of, 30
Enabling power, 74
Endowment: and God's presence, 11, 41; and embodiment of Christ, 13; rejected by Israel, 20; received by early Saints, 27; clothing and ritual elements of, 36–37, 38–39, 59–60; author's preparation for, 42–43; and baptismal covenants, 50; covenants of, 51; as gift, 51–52, 74; and Freemasonry, 66–68; and receiving redemption, 73; changes to, 74–77; of priesthood power, 77–79; as private, 79–80; and priesthood offices, 79–81; purpose of, 108; and ascension, 113
Eternal life, 40, 48
Exaltation, 79, 85, 86, 88
Experiential knowledge, 39–40
Eyring, Henry B., 85–86

Faith: in God's faithfulness, 29–30; as foundation of covenant path, 85–86; in Jesus Christ, 106; unto repentance, 106–7; sources of, 107–8
Family relationship, in covenants, 18–20
Fire of the covenant, 27–28
Food, 36

Freemasonry, 65–68
Fruit, of tree of life, 40–43

Garment, 55–56, 59, 62, 63, 64. *See also* clothing
Gifts, of endowment, 51–52, 74
Glory, degrees of, 57, 78, 86, 90, 91
God: presence of, 6, 7–8, 10–12, 20–22, 25, 30–31, 39, 41, 88, 90, 97, 98–99; covenants and identity and name of, 17; and temple as house of Lord, 23–31; becoming like, 24–25, 47–48; faith in promises of, 29–30; knowing, 40; seeking, 40–45; serving, 58; being cut off from, 71; drawing close to, 99–101
Godliness, 24–25, 84–85
Gō'ēl, 18–19
Gong, Gerrit W., 89
Good thing, laying hold upon every, 104–5
Gospel, fullness of, 95–97, 97–99, 101–2

Hinckley, Gordon B., 95–96
Holiness: and Old Testament temple structure, 8–11; through offerings and rituals, 12–13
Holland, Jeffrey R., 13, 32, 54, 70
Holy Ghost, 21
Holy of Holies, 10
Home, impact of temple attendance on, 27
House of the Lord, 23–31
Hunter, Howard W., 108, 109, 110

Identity, new, 57
Inheritance, 64
Initiatory ordinance, 38
Islam, 36
Israel, 7–8, 15, 18, 20, 30. *See also* Old Testament temple

INDEX

Jacob, 16, 17
Jesus Christ: coming unto, 1, 2, 6–7, 14, 73; anointing of, 5–6; focusing on, 6, 85–86; ordinances pointing to, 12–13; and need for temple, 13–14; covenant relationship with, 18–20; redemption through, 19, 71–72, 86, 107; and temple as house of Lord, 23–31; appears in Kirtland Temple, 26; manifestation of, 26–27; and covenant path, 48–49; baptism of, 50; "putting on," 56–57, 62–63; new life in, 57–59; taking upon name of, 60, 85; becoming like, 62, 108–9; giving ourselves to, 64; and new and everlasting covenant, 83–84; covenant order of, 86–88; sanctification through, 90–91; bridges gap between us and God, 100–101; choosing and receiving, 104–5; transformation through, 105–6; faith in, 106; knowing, 110–11; taking upon yoke of, 112–13. *See also* Atonement
Jewish religious practice, 34–36

Kimball, Heber, 66
Kimball, Spencer W., 105–6
Kirtland Temple, 25, 26–27
Knowledge: ritual, in Old Testament, 39–40; covenant, 112–13

Law of Moses, 20, 40, 61
Lee, Harold B., 50, 52–53, 77
Lehi's dream, 40–43
Life, newness of, 57–59
Light of Christ, 99, 100, 104
Liturgy, 37–39
Lusts, 62–63

Marriage, 84–86. *See also* new and everlasting covenant
Masonry, 65–68
McKay, David O., 106
Mecca, 36
Meekness, 111
Melchizedek Priesthood, 8–9, 20–21, 24, 78–79
Messengers, authorized, 69
Mortality, 69
Moses, 17, 20, 60–61
Muslims, 36

Names, and covenants, 16–17, 19
Nature, changing, 53–54
Nauvoo Temple, 24, 27
Nelson, Russell M.: and understanding temple ordinances, 2; on temple covenants, 16, 110; on gathering of Israel, 30; on covenant path, 48; on women and priesthood power, 60, 80–81; on coming unto God, 73; on changes in temple ordinances, 76–77, 82; on Melchizedek priesthood blessings, 78; on priesthood ordinances, 80; on understanding covenants and ordinances, 82; on mission of Church, 92; on Book of Mormon, 95; on power of God and Christ, 100; on temple worship, 107; on temple attendance, 110; on temple construction, 110
New and everlasting covenant, 83–84; and marriage and godliness, 84–85; and focusing on Christ, 85–86; and order of priesthood, 86–88; and trials, 88–89; and abiding in covenants, 89–90; and sanctification through

INDEX

Christ, 90–91; receiving, 99–101

Oaks, Dallin H., 45–46, 99, 103

Offerings, 12–13

Old Testament, ritual knowledge in, 39–40

Old Testament temple: structure of, 8–11; entry into, 11–12. *See also* tabernacle

Ordinances: holiness and wholeness through, 12–13; putting on Christ through, 56–58; changes to, 74–77, 81–82; and entering God's order, 86, 87; point to power of Atonement, 97–99; vicarious, 99–102; and repentance, 107; and spiritual rebirth, 111. *See also* ritual(s)

Orientation, ritual as, 33–34

Packer, Boyd K., 12

Pioneers, 27–28

Plan of salvation, 15, 16, 18, 69–70, 92–93, 99–102

Poor, care for, 28

Practice, and belief, 94–95, 98

Priesthood: and temple covenants, 15, 20, 24; and temple blessings, 43–45; order of, 86–88. *See also* Aaronic Priesthood; Melchizedek Priesthood

Priesthood keys, restoration of, 26–27

Priesthood offices, 79–81

Priesthood power, 77–79

Priests, 9–10, 11–13, 59, 60, 61, 63–64

Questions, 1–2

Rasband, Ronald A., 8

Recommends, for entering temple, 7–8

Redemption: covenants and, 18–20; through Christ, 19, 71–72, 86, 107. *See also* salvation

Religious practice, ritual and, 34–37

Repentance, 94, 106–7

Restoration, as process, 75–77, 78

Revelation, 69, 104

Ritual(s), 32; holiness and wholeness through, 12–13; and worship and becoming, 33; as orientation, 33–34; and religious practice, 34–37; and liturgy and worship, 37–39; in Old Testament, 39–40; in Lehi's dream, 40–43; and discipleship, 45–46. *See also* ordinances

Rouché, President and Sister, 42

Sabbath, 36

Sacrifice(s): animal, 12, 75; of broken heart and contrite spirit, 61, 62–63; offered by Adam and Eve, 70–71

Salvation, 47, 73, 79. *See also* redemption

Sanctification, 90–91

Sarah, 16, 29

Satan, 71, 82

Sealing ordinance, 84

Service, 40, 80

Sin, remission of, 94

Smith, Joseph, 25, 65–67, 76

Smith, Joseph F., 101

Spiritual progress, 73, 113–14. *See also* change

Spirit world, gospel message shared in, 101, 103. *See also* afterlife

Suffering, 114

Tabernacle, 1, 60–61. *See also* Old Testament temple

Telestial kingdom, 90

Temple: coming unto Christ through, 1, 2, 6–7, 14; finding

INDEX

answers in, 1–2; purpose of, 5–7, 17, 24–25; worthiness to enter, 7–8; offerings and rituals in, 12–13; need for, 13–14; and covenants, 15–22; commandments to build, 23–24; as house of Lord, 23–31; and Freemasonry, 65–68; blessings of, 107; and becoming like Christ, 108–9. *See also* Kirtland Temple; Nauvoo Temple; Old Testament temple

Temple attendance, frequency of, 109–10
Temple blessings, 43–45, 110–11
Temple clothing, 38
Temple garment, 55–56, 59, 62, 63, 64
Temple recommends, 7–8
Temple veil, 10

Tertullian, 94
Time, ritual and orientation to, 36
Transformation. *See* change; spiritual progress
Tree of life, fruit of, 40–43
Trials, 88–89
Truth, 95–97

Veil, 10

Washing and anointing, 38
Wayward children, 86
Wilcox, Brad, 30–31
Will / willingness: to follow covenant path, 52–53; aligning with God's, 54
Women, 79, 80–81
World, living in, 45–46
Worship, 33, 37–39, 40, 61–62
Worthiness, to enter temple, 7–8

Young, Brigham, 28, 74, 96, 114

LET'S TALK ABOUT...

FAITH-AFFIRMING EXPLORATIONS ON A VARIETY OF CHALLENGING TOPICS

LET'S TALK ABOUT TEMPLES AND RITUAL
JENNIFER C. LANE

LET'S TALK ABOUT THE TRANSLATION OF THE BOOK OF MORMON
GERRIT J. DIRKMAAT
MICHAEL HUBBARD MACKAY
NEW!

LET'S TALK ABOUT RACE AND PRIESTHOOD
W. PAUL REEVE
FOREWORD BY DARIUS A. GRAY
NEW!

LET'S TALK ABOUT FAITH AND INTELLECT
TERRYL GIVENS
NEW!

LET'S TALK ABOUT THE LAW OF CONSECRATION
STEVEN C. HARPER

LET'S TALK ABOUT THE BOOK OF ABRAHAM
KERRY MUHLESTEIN

LET'S TALK ABOUT RELIGION AND MENTAL HEALTH
DANIEL K JUDD

LET'S TALK ABOUT POLYGAMY
BRITTANY CHAPMAN NASH

MORE TITLES COMING SOON!

Visit desbook.com/letstalk to complete your collection